D0065386

JACKIE ROBINSON

JACKIE ROBINSON

A Biography

Mary Kay Linge

GREENWOOD BIOGRAPHIES

GREENWOOD PRESS
WESTPORT, CONNECTICUT • LONDON

Library of Congress Cataloging-in-Publication Data

Linge, Mary Kay.
    Jackie Robinson : a biography / by Mary Kay Linge.
        p. cm. — (Greenwood biographies, ISSN 1540–4900)
    Includes bibliographical references and index.
    ISBN-13: 978–0–313–33828–1 (alk. paper)
    ISBN-10: 0–313–33828–0 (alk. paper)
    1. Robinson, Jackie, 1919–1972. 2. Baseball players—United States—
Biography. 3. African American baseball players—Biography. I. Title.
    GV865.R6L56   2007
    796.357092—dc22
    [B]   2007009619

British Library Cataloguing in Publication Data is available.

Library of Congress Catalog Card Number: 2007009619
ISBN-13: 978–0–313–33828–1
ISBN-10: 0–313–33828–0
ISSN: 1540–4900

First published in 2007

Greenwood Press, 88 Post Road West, Westport, CT 06881
An imprint of Greenwood Publishing Group, Inc.
www.greenwood.com

Printed in the United States of America

The paper used in this book complies with the
Permanent Paper Standard issued by the National
Information Standards Organization (Z39.48–1984).

10 9 8 7 6 5 4 3 2 1

CONTENTS

Photo essay follows page 70.

SERIES FOREWORD

In response to high school and public library needs, Greenwood developed this distinguished series of full-length biographies specifically for student use. Prepared by field experts and professionals, these engaging biographies are tailored for high school students who need challenging yet accessible biographies. Ideal for secondary school assignments, the length, format and subject areas are designed to meet educators' requirements and students' interests.

Greenwood offers an extensive selection of biographies spanning all curriculum-related subject areas including social studies, the sciences, literature and the arts, history and politics, as well as popular culture, covering public figures and famous personalities from all time periods and backgrounds, both historic and contemporary, who have made an impact on American and/or world culture. Greenwood biographies were chosen based on comprehensive feedback from librarians and educators. Consideration was given to both curriculum relevance and inherent interest. The result is an intriguing mix of the well known and the unexpected, the saints and sinners from long-ago history and contemporary pop culture. Readers will find a wide array of subject choices from fascinating crime figures like Al Capone to inspiring pioneers like Margaret Mead, from the greatest minds of our time like Stephen Hawking to the most amazing success stories of our day like J. K. Rowling.

While the emphasis is on fact, not glorification, the books are meant to be fun to read. Each volume provides in-depth information about the subject's life from birth through childhood, the teen years, and adulthood.

A thorough account relates family background and education, traces personal and professional influences, and explores struggles, accomplishments, and contributions. A timeline highlights the most significant life events against a historical perspective. Bibliographies supplement the reference value of each volume.

INTRODUCTION

The importance of Jackie Robinson's life is almost impossible to overstate. At a time when most of American society was segregated either by law or by custom, Robinson, as the first black baseball player in the modern history of "America's pastime," blazed a new path and proved to the nation that there could be another way.

Robinson's success, historians contend, reached far beyond baseball to prepare the ground for the coming Civil Rights Movement. And as many ballplayers have said, at the time and since, Robinson's character and background made him the perfect—perhaps the only—man for the job.

A champion in every sport he tried, Robinson was a driven competitor but also a great team player. College educated, he could hold his own with the media. He had played on integrated teams for most of his life, but his experience in the U.S. Army and in baseball's Negro Leagues had given him enough exposure to segregation for him to know what he would be up against. Morally upright and a committed Christian, he had a sense of mission about his life that allowed him to take terrible abuse from bigots and racists. He was also fiercely devoted to victory for his team; along with his passionate style of play, Robinson became known for his strongly worded protests to umpires and opponents on the field (after spending his first two big-league seasons in silent forbearance).

In his post-baseball life, he was criticized by some whites for being too militant on civil rights, and by some blacks for being too accommodating. For his part, Robinson maintained that he remained himself, always: it was the society around him, and the image that others held of him, that changed. In his own eyes, it was his sense of righteousness (which, to others, sometimes turned into self-righteousness) that sustained him in the fight to integrate baseball and beyond.

Robinson was not the first black man to play major league baseball. In the 1880s, as the National League formed, a handful of African American players competed alongside whites on a few of the earliest major league teams. But when racial attitudes hardened into legalized segregation in the South and white stars like Cap Anson refused to take the field with black ballplayers, baseball adopted an informal "gentleman's agreement" barring blacks from the major leagues.

By the 1940s, Negro League baseball had produced dozens of talented ballplayers who regularly played—and beat—white major leaguers in post-season barnstorming games. African American soldiers had fought with distinction in World War II, and laborers of all races had worked side by side in the war effort. Baseball's color line was beginning to seem antique to many fans, sportswriters, and club owners.

It was Branch Rickey, president and general manager of the Brooklyn Dodgers, who took the decisive step to break baseball's racial barriers. One of the game's great innovators, Rickey realized that the Negro Leagues harbored an untapped pool of baseball talent, and that the first club in would have its pick of the best players. A religious man, he also believed that integration was simply the right thing to do.

Still, Rickey understood that a pioneering black major leaguer would have a painful and difficult path. Decades of racism and segregation would not melt away from baseball overnight. Rickey had to find an excellent ballplayer with unimpeachable morals and a respectable background who could be tough enough to bear all kinds of abuse and strong enough to resist the urge to react to it. These exacting requirements were fulfilled by Jackie Robinson.

Born in the strictly segregated South, Robinson grew up in equally, but less obviously, segregated Pasadena, California. He watched his older brother Mack gain international fame as an Olympic silver medalist, then return home to the only local job he could get: as a street sweeper. Robinson fought for equality as an Army lieutenant during World War II to the point of being court-martialed for his refusal to move to the back of a bus at Camp Hood, Texas.

Robinson's own athletic abilities were recognized early, and he gained a national reputation in football as a halfback for the UCLA Bruins. Baseball was just one of the sports in which he excelled, but for an African American it provided the only opportunity for a career as a professional athlete. After the war, Robinson joined the Kansas City Monarchs, one of the premier teams in Negro League baseball.

His single season with the Monarchs got him noticed by Rickey and the Dodgers. Rickey seized on sportswriters' and scouts' reports about Robinson, noting not only his baseball skills, but also his background as a college-educated former Army officer. The Dodger president believed that Robinson had the poise and self-control necessary to stand up to certain abuse—and have, as Rickey put it, "guts enough *not* to fight back."

The 1947 season was a watershed for Robinson, for baseball, and for the entire country as African Americans finally claimed their rightful place on the fields of America's most popular sport. Within weeks, the American League's Cleveland Indians were integrated, too.

Robinson, as the standard bearer, endured death threats, rumored players' boycotts, abysmal segregated accommodations, on-field taunts, and almost unendurable stress. With his wife Rachel's support, and with the steadfast backing of teammates like Pee Wee Reese, Robinson not only survived in major league baseball, he thrived. In his first season, he hit .297, scored 125 runs, and stole a league-leading 29 bases, winning Rookie of the Year honors and helping his team capture the National League pennant. At the same time he transformed the game, using speed on the basepaths as an offensive weapon and bringing Negro League–style daring into play.

In his ten-year career with the Dodgers, Robinson compiled a .311 batting average, appeared in six All-Star games, and was named the league's Most Valuable Player (MVP). For Brooklyn fans, though, his greatest accomplishment was his position as a leader of the world champion 1955 team, capped by his thrilling steal of home in a World Series game against the New York Yankees.

Robinson's retirement in 1957 was the end of an era. The Dodgers played one final year in Brooklyn, then moved to Los Angeles as major-league baseball expanded cross-country. Jackie Robinson came to epitomize the Brooklyn club of the 1950s: tough, competitive, team-oriented, triumphant.

After his retirement, Robinson threw himself into the fight for civil rights, giving speeches, raising funds, writing syndicated newspaper columns, and working with Martin Luther King Jr. and other black leaders to end segregation and extend equal opportunity to all Americans. He angered some activists with his political support of Republicans like Richard Nixon and Nelson Rockefeller, but Robinson believed that party affiliation was meaningless compared to a politician's commitment to equality.

Robinson's health declined sharply in the 1960s, as diabetes—probably stress-induced—took a heavy toll. His induction into the Baseball Hall of Fame in 1962 was a high point, but business disappointments and political disillusionment made his health woes more difficult to bear. His oldest son's descent into drug abuse after military service in Vietnam was a nightmare for the Robinson family. They supported Jackie Junior as he worked through rehabilitation programs and became a drug counselor himself, but the young man's sudden death in a car crash was a tragedy from which Robinson never recovered.

In 1973, a quarter-century after Robinson broke the color line, baseball could put his achievements into perspective, and Robinson himself was able to let go of the remaining bitterness he felt toward the game. The Dodgers retired his uniform number, 42, in a Los Angeles ceremony that Robinson attended, and Robinson was asked to throw out the ceremonial first pitch in a World Series game that fall. Contentious to the end, he declared at the game that he would not be truly happy until baseball hired a black coach or field manager. He did not live to see Frank Robinson achieve that goal with the Cleveland Indians in 1975.

Jackie Robinson died of a heart attack on October 24, 1973. Thousands turned out to mourn him at his funeral in Harlem.

After his death, baseball and the nation continued to honor him with posthumous awards. Perhaps the most significant of these came on April 15, 1997, 50 years after his historic Dodgers debut, when Robinson's uniform number was retired by every team in Major League Baseball. No ballplayer can ever again wear number 42, in memory of the life and the accomplishments of Jackie Robinson. He is the only player to be so honored, a singular achievement for a singular figure in American history.

TIMELINE: EVENTS IN THE LIFE OF JACKIE ROBINSON

1919   Jack Roosevelt Robinson is born on January 31 near Cairo, Georgia, the fifth and youngest child of Jerry Robinson and Mallie McGriff Robinson.

1920   Robinson is taken to live in California by his mother and siblings; they settle with other family members in Pasadena.

1935–1936   Robinson plays quarterback for his champion high-school football team.

1936   Robinson's brother Mack wins the silver medal in the 200 meters at the Olympic Games in Berlin.

1937–1938   Robinson stars in football, track, basketball, and baseball at Pasadena Junior College.

1939   Recruited by the University of California–Los Angeles (UCLA), Robinson joins their football team and gains national recognition at halfback; he also excels in basketball, track, and baseball, becoming UCLA's first four-letter man.

1940   Robinson wins the NCAA broad-jump championship; he begins dating Rachel Isum, a fellow UCLA student.

1941   Robinson drops out of UCLA in his final semester to take a job with the federal government's National Youth Administration.

1942   Months after the attack on Pearl Harbor, Robinson is drafted into the U.S. Army; he meets and

befriends boxing champ Joe Louis when both are
stationed at Fort Riley in Kansas.

1943   Robinson is commissioned as a second lieutenant.

1944   Court-martialed when refuses to move to the back
of a bus at Camp Hood, Texas, Robinson is acquitted,
then honorably discharged from the military.

1945   Robinson plays shortstop for the Kansas City
Monarchs of the Negro National League.
On October 23, Robinson formally signs a
contract to play baseball for the Brooklyn Dodgers
organization; he agrees to the condition set by
Dodgers president Branch Rickey that he will have
the "guts enough not to fight back" against taunting
and bigotry on and off the field.

1946   Robinson and Rachel Isum are married on
February 10.
With the champion Montreal Royals of the
International League, Robinson becomes the first
black man to play "organized" baseball in the
twentieth century and earns the league MVP award
with his league-leading .349 batting average.
Son Jackie Junior is born on November 18.

1947   In spring training, an anti-integration petition is
circulated among some Dodger players and quickly
squelched by manager Leo Durocher.
On April 15, Robinson debuts as the Brooklyn
Dodgers' first baseman to become the first black
major leaguer in the modern history of baseball;
at least one opposing team threatens to strike, but
instead opponents resort to vicious race-baiting
on the field; Robinson receives both death threats
and accolades from fans.
Robinson has an outstanding rookie season,
batting .297 with a league-leading 29 stolen bases
and a momentum-turning base running style; he is
named the first-ever Rookie of the Year and helps
Dodgers win the National League pennant.

1948   Robinson moves to second base, forming one of
baseball's great double-play combinations with
shortstop Pee Wee Reese.

After more than two seasons of on-field silence, Robinson begins to argue calls with umpires and shout at opponents from the bench, allowing his true competitive spirit to emerge.

1949 Fans elect Robinson to the National League All-Star team for the first of his six appearances; he is the first black All-Star, along with Roy Campanella, Don Newcombe, and Larry Doby, who also appear in the contest on July 12.
Robinson testifies before the House Un-American Activities Committee of the U.S. Congress on July 18 to affirm the patriotism of African Americans.
In August, the song "Did You See Jackie Robinson Hit That Ball?" rises to number 13 on the pop charts.
Robinson is named the National League MVP with a league-leading .342 batting average, 37 stolen bases, 124 RBI, and 122 runs scored; the Dodgers win the pennant.

1950 Daughter Sharon is born on January 13.
Robinson stars as himself in an autobiographical movie, *The Jackie Robinson Story*, filmed during the off-season and released in May.

1951 In the "Miracle of Coogan's Bluff," the New York Giants defeat the Dodgers with a walk-off Bobby Thomson home run that gives them the National League pennant; in an impressive show of good sportsmanship, Robinson is the only Dodger to visit the Giants clubhouse and congratulate them.

1952 Son David is born on May 14.
Robinson gets his 1,000th career hit on August 9; Brooklyn wins the National League pennant.
Robinson accuses the New York Yankees of racism in a postseason television interview.

1953 The Dodgers take the National League pennant again and again lose the World Series to the Yankees.

1954 In perhaps the worst on-field blowup of his career, Robinson argues repeatedly with an umpire and is tossed from a game in Milwaukee on June 2; he accidentally throws his bat into the stands and injures a fan.

The Robinson family moves out of New York City to Stamford, Connecticut, drawing criticism from those who feel the all-white suburb is "not their place."

1955   The Dodgers win the World Series, for the first and only time in the team's 75-year history in Brooklyn; Robinson's steal of home in Game One is a momentum-shifting factor in the series.

1956   The NAACP awards the Springarn Medal, its highest honor, to Robinson for his distinguished service to the African American people.

Robinson is traded to cross-town rival New York Giants in December, stunning the baseball world.

1957   Robinson announces his retirement from baseball, refusing to play for the Giants; he takes a job as an executive with the Chock full o'Nuts company.

Robinson joins the Civil Rights Movement in earnest, speaking and fundraising on behalf of the NAACP.

Robinson is diagnosed with diabetes, brought on in part by the stress of his fight to integrate baseball.

1958   Increasingly vocal on the matter of school integration, Robinson serves as marshal of the Youth March for Integrated Schools in Washington, DC.

1959   Robinson launches a syndicated newspaper column in which he opines on sports, politics, and social issues.

1960   Entering presidential politics, Robinson campaigns for Hubert Humphrey in the Democratic primaries; in the general election he endorses Richard M. Nixon over John F. Kennedy due to his belief that the Republican is more committed to civil rights.

1962   Robinson is inducted into the National Baseball Hall of Fame in his first year of eligibility.

1963   The Robinsons host the Afternoon of Jazz fundraiser at their home for Martin Luther King's

Southern Christian Leadership Conference
(SCLC), the first in an ongoing series of fundraising
events sponsored by the Robinson family.
Robinson and his family participate in the historic
March on Washington on August 28.
Malcolm X and Robinson argue about integration
and black separatism via "open letters" printed in
Robinson's newspaper column.

1964   Robinson resigns from Chock full o'Nuts to join
Nelson Rockefeller's unsuccessful campaign for the
Republican presidential nomination.
Freedom National Bank, a black-owned bank
with Robinson as chairman of the board, opens in
Harlem.

1965   After a year of U.S. Army training, Jackie Junior is
sent to fight in Vietnam.

1966   Robinson joins the staff of New York's Governor
Rockefeller as a community affairs aide.

1968   Jackie Junior is arrested for drug and weapons
possession; he enters a rehabilitation program to
treat his heroin addiction.
Martin Luther King Jr. is assassinated, leaving
Robinson "bitterly disillusioned."
Robinson leaves Rockefeller's staff to campaign for
Democrat Hubert Humphrey against Nixon in the
presidential election campaign.

1971   Now heroin-free and a drug treatment counselor,
Jackie Junior is killed in a car crash.

1973   The Los Angeles Dodgers retire Robinson's
uniform number, 42, in a June 4 ceremony that he
attends.
Baseball celebrates the 25th anniversary of
Robinson's major-league debut at Game Two of
the World Series in Cincinnati; Robinson throws
out the first pitch in his last public appearance.
Robinson dies of a heart attack on October
24; thousands mourn him at funeral services at
Riverside Church in New York City; he is buried
in Brooklyn.

Chapter 1

CHILDHOOD, 1919–1936

"You might say that I turned professional at an early age," Jackie Robinson would say, because even as a small child he was paid for his athletic abilities. In his early school days, other boys would give him "sandwiches and dimes for the movies so they could play on my team."[1]

The food he collected this way made a real difference, because in the mid-1920s the Robinson family was just scraping by. Mallie Robinson was rearing her five children alone, a continent away from her birthplace, and every dime and morsel helped. All the Robinson children, even baby-of-the-family Jackie, were well aware of that. At the age of six or eight, when he went to school, "I told my mother she could save food by not fixing a lunch for me," instead collecting his own meals from his schoolmates. "I had to win from the start if I wanted to eat as well as the rest of my friends."[2]

Jackie Robinson was born to sharecroppers who lived on a large farm near Cairo, Georgia. His mother, Mallie McGriff, was a member of a prosperous local black family. Her father, Wash, and her mother, Edna, had both been born into slavery. After the Civil War ended, they had worked hard in the difficult Reconstruction years to acquire their own piece of farmland. Education was tremendously important to the McGriffs and all 14 of the family's children grew up with the idea that schooling was a necessary part of a better life. Mallie, the seventh child, was born in 1892. She attended school through the sixth grade, a great achievement for the time. At the age of 10 she repaid her father's lifetime of effort by teaching him how to read the Bible.[3]

When Mallie married, it was for love—and her choice was a disappointment to her family. Jerry Robinson was an uneducated laborer who lived on, but did not own, the land he worked. The grandson of slaves, Jerry was one of 11 children. He had lived his whole life on the Sasser plantation, where the Robinsons were sharecroppers. Like many other black families in Georgia at the time, they farmed a portion of the land in exchange for a fraction—a share—of the crop they grew. Jerry himself was a paid laborer who worked for wages of less than $12 a month.

Mallie, who was 14 years old when they met, was entranced by Jerry's smile and flattered by his attention. Her parents tried to deflect her interest, but Mallie insisted that Jerry was the one for her. They married in 1909, when Mallie was 17 and Jerry was 21, and moved into a cabin on the Sasser farm.

Mallie's fierce will emerged immediately, when she argued that Jerry should have a better deal with the landowner, Jim Sasser. Sasser was a large and intimidating man who strove to control every detail of his tenant farmers' lives, dictating where they could shop (at Sasser's own store, naturally) and whether they could accept work away from the plantation. But Jerry Robinson was one of Sasser's most reliable laborers, and he could not risk losing the young man. Mallie pushed Jerry to demand a half-cropping arrangement, in which he would keep a full half of whatever he might grow or raise on his assigned land, and Sasser agreed. The landowner would provide a house for them to live in, land for them to work, seed, and fertilizer. Half their crop would belong to Sasser, and the rest would be the Robinsons' to use or to sell as they pleased.

With that incentive to drive them, Mallie and Jerry set to work. Mallie, energetic and resourceful, was soon raising her own hogs, chickens, and turkeys, as well as vegetables. Jerry farmed the rich land well, and it yielded cotton, sugar cane, peanuts, potatoes, and corn. Their income more than doubled, from $134 a year to about $350.[4] As their children came—beginning with Edgar in 1910—Mallie was content. "We were just living as I wanted to live,"[5] she would remember.

But Jerry was restless. After a few seasons of half-cropping, with extra money in his pocket for the first time in his life, he began to enjoy spending time and cash in the nearby city of Cairo. Mallie preferred life on the farm. For several years they cycled between separation and reconciliation. Rumors flew of other women in Jerry's life, but Mallie, inspired by her deepening religious faith, repeatedly forgave him. Then another child would be born—Frank in 1911, Mack in 1914, and Willa Mae in 1916. They would stay together for a time, but eventually Jerry would leave again.

He was with Mallie on the evening of January 31, 1919 when she gave birth to a healthy boy. The parents named him Jack Roosevelt Robinson in honor of former president Teddy Roosevelt, who had died earlier that month.

Six months later Jerry was gone yet again, claiming to be heading for Texas. Family stories vary as to whether he planned to seek work there or to visit a brother. The local rumor mill generated stories that Jerry had in fact headed north, or perhaps south to Florida, accompanied by a married neighbor with whom he had been having a long-running affair. Whatever his intentions, Jerry Robinson was gone for good, and his youngest son never heard from him again. Jackie Robinson would remain bitter about his father's abandonment until the end of his life.[6]

Jim Sasser was furious at this development, and he put the blame on Mallie—for insisting on the half-cropping deal, for not keeping hold of her husband, and perhaps most of all for her self-possession and lack of fear. (When Sasser offered to send the county sheriff after Jerry, she refused to allow it, noting that her husband was "a free man, free to do what he wanted."[7]) The landowner evicted her and the children from their tenant cottage and placed them in a small, unpleasant cabin. And he still expected her to bring in the summer's crops.

THE ROBINSONS HEAD WEST

Mallie soon realized there was little chance of a better future, for herself or for her children, in Georgia. The summer of 1919, which became known as the "Red Summer," was marked by more than 20 violent race riots in cities from Chicago to Washington, DC to Charleston, South Carolina. At least 100 blacks were killed in these clashes, which were sparked as white soldiers returning from Europe after World War I found themselves competing with blacks for scarce jobs. The riots heightened racial tensions nationwide, and especially in Georgia, where lynchings were frighteningly common. When her half-brother Burton Thomas came back to Cairo for a visit, Mallie saw a way out.

Burton had left for California several years before, and he had prospered there, working as a gardener for well-off families in the Los Angeles suburbs. He owned a house in Pasadena, and he encouraged his Georgia relatives to consider following him west. The McGriffs decided that a contingent of the family would do just that. They pooled their cash to buy 13 train tickets, enough for Mallie's family, the family of her sister Cora Wade, and their brother Paul McGriff to leave for Los Angeles. In late May of 1920, 16-month-old Jackie Robinson was carried aboard a California-bound train.

When the group reached Pasadena, they rented a small, three-room apartment for the Robinson and Wade families to share. Mallie quickly found work as a domestic servant, cooking and cleaning for a well-to-do white family in Pasadena. She helped support her extended family with her wages, while her sister Cora cared for the younger children. They remained in the apartment for a short time, then moved into Burton Thomas's home on Glorietta Street in the northwest part of town, where most of Pasadena's black residents lived.

Pasadena had a growing black population, but as Jackie Robinson would write later, the city "regarded us as intruders."[8] The Robinsons had left the segregation laws of the Jim Crow South behind them, but they quickly found that the races in California were also kept separate, by force of custom if not by law. Certain parts of town were known as "white" or as "black" areas, for example, and landlords and real-estate agents would simply not rent or sell to the "wrong sort of people." Town ordinances and local businesses also contributed to a sort of patchwork segregation: movie theaters steered black patrons to the balcony or to side seating sections, and the public swimming pool in Brookside Park permitted blacks in the water only one day per week—after which the pool was emptied, cleaned, and refilled. As a result, whites and blacks in Pasadena were largely separated in their day-to-day lives, and opportunities for black workers and students were severely limited.

The house on Glorietta Street was comfortable and roomy, but the arrangement could not last for long—Burton Thomas was not accustomed to children and had a difficult time living with seven of them. In 1922, the Robinsons and Wades jointly bought a house of their own at 121 Pepper Street, on an all-white block. Barely three years old, Jackie Robinson was already a pioneer.

There remains some question about how Mallie Robinson and the Wades managed to purchase their own home on what were undoubtedly limited salaries. One biographer suggests that the Robinsons were the beneficiaries of a real-estate scheme in which a black broker sold the home to them at a cut rate, hoping that the sudden appearance of a black family would make local whites panic and clamor to buy the house away from them at double or triple its value.[9]

If this was the plan, it didn't work: the Robinson family would own and live in the house on Pepper Street for decades. In part, this was due to their efforts to prove themselves as good neighbors, despite the white residents' initial opposition. As Willa Mae described it, "We went through a sort of slavery, with the whites slowly, very slowly, getting used to us."[10] Harassment ranged from the cross that someone burned on their front lawn one night to shouts of "Nigger, nigger" from neighboring kids to the near-daily noise complaints that were lodged against the Robinson children. (The sound of 12-year-old Edgar roller-skating down the sidewalk was apparently most annoying.)

Mallie Robinson's faith in God inspired her and her family during this difficult time, and it offered an outlook that her youngest son would adopt as an adult. Mallie "didn't allow us to go out of our way to antagonize the whites," Jackie Robinson would write later, "and she still made it perfectly clear to us and to them...that she had no intention of allowing them to mistreat us."[11] Instead, Mallie chose to love her neighbors, as the Bible instructed. She made sure that Edgar ran errands and did odd jobs for Clara Coppersmith, an elderly widow who had initially been fiercely opposed to the idea of living next door to a black family. Soon the influential Mrs. Coppersmith became the Robinsons' defender, quashing a petition drive to get them out of their house. A local baker allowed the Robinson boys to collect his unsold bread and cookies each Saturday evening, and Mallie boxed the items up for the children to share with neighbors. "At first, when we went to them, they couldn't figure it out," Willa Mae remembered, "but then that changed them."[12]

The family took great pride in the house itself, with its five bedrooms, two bathrooms, and large yard. Several kinds of fruit trees thrived there, and the Robinsons and Wades planted flower beds and a vegetable garden as well. As she had done back in Georgia, Mallie raised fowl and even rabbits to help feed her family.

This kind of self-sufficiency was necessary because money was tight, even though by this time all the adults in the household worked. There were days when the children's only meals consisted of leftovers Mallie brought home from her job. When food was that scarce, young Jackie "could never get my belt tight enough to keep that hurt in my stomach away."[13]

With their only parent working long hours every day, the Robinson siblings had to care for one another at an early age. Mallie was often away from the home, but her expectations for her children were crystal clear: they were to attend school without fail, complete their homework every day, devote each Sunday to God, and help the family any way they could.

That meant, in part, that each child was responsible for the well-being of the next youngest, so when Willa Mae was five or six and Jackie about three, she became his primary caregiver. She dressed him, fed him, bathed him, and even took him along to Grover Cleveland Elementary School with her each day. Then she left her little brother to play alone in the schoolyard sandbox, since Jackie was too young to attend school himself. Willa Mae would watch over her brother during lessons from her classroom window, running out to him if he needed any help. In bad weather, the boy was allowed to stay in the kindergarten classroom until dismissal time.[14]

The sandbox arrangement was unorthodox, to say the least, and although the kind-hearted Cleveland School teachers had agreed to it, their higher-ups complained. As usual, Mallie was forthright and spoke up. "If I quit working to stay home to take care of him, I'll have to go on relief," she reasoned with the school authorities; "it'll be cheaper for the city if you just let him play in the sandbox."[15] Her logic was undeniable. She got her way.

At home, meanwhile, Jackie imitated the play of his older siblings. His brother Mack remembered that all the Robinson children loved speed and movement; they became infamous in the neighborhood for their habit of hurtling along the sidewalks on bikes or skates at terrifying velocities. Little Jackie was no exception. As Mack recalled, the first indication he had that his brother would become a great athlete came when "he was about three years old and he owned a tricycle. One of his greatest joys was hopping on that tricycle and speeding around chairs like a hot-rodder" all around the house. "Even then, his judgment was keen, and he had good balance."[16]

Once he was old enough to leave the sandbox and join the kindergarten class inside the building, Jackie's athletic skills soon became just as well known at school. Not only did kids "pay" him with snacks and pocket change to play on their teams, at Cleveland Elementary he made several of his lifelong friends, including Ray Bartlett and Sid Heard, who shared his taste for sports.

In the third or fourth grade, Jackie played forward on a soccer team made up of boys in his class. They were so good "we challenged the sixth grade team and beat them. After that, we represented the school in matches."[17] By now he was enrolled at Washington Elementary School, along with a large proportion of Pasadena's black children. This was a deliberate move by the city, whose leaders had taken note of the influx of black and Hispanic families and had altered the school zoning to create, in effect, a segregated education system.

These racial politics went completely unnoticed by Jack, whose life at this age was driven by sports, and by the need to win, whatever the game. "He was good at any game he took up,"[18] Ray Bartlett would recall—marbles, handball, soccer, dodge-ball, golf. At the same time, other boyhood friends would later say that Jack's intense focus on winning made him hard to like.[19]

To Jack, though, sports had another meaning as well: they were "the big breach in the wall of segregation about me. In primary and high school white boys treated me like an equal." Southern California's mild climate allowed him to pursue athletics all year round; Pasadena's prosperity meant that fields and playing facilities were easily available. "The more

I played the better I became—in softball, hard ball, football, basketball, tennis, table tennis, any kind of game with a ball."[20]

Outside of sports and school, as a preteen, Jack became part of an informal group of neighborhood boys who called themselves the "Pepper Street Gang." "We had all colors and creeds," he would say in later years. "There were Mexicans and Japanese kids as well as Negroes."[21] The boys' activities were mischievous, at times bordering on the criminal; in a generally peaceful city like Pasadena, they attracted a good deal of interest from the police. The boys stole fruit from local orchards or stores, threw mud at cars as they passed by, and shoplifted.[22] A favorite pastime was lurking in the roughs at the city's new public golf course and stealing stray balls as the golfers searched for them. Often the boys would proceed to sell the balls back to their original owners.[23]

The head of the police department's youth division, Captain Hugh D. Morgan, became a regular visitor to the Robinson household, and the visits sometimes went both ways—Mallie Robinson would on occasion head to the police station and scold Morgan when she thought his enforcement measures had gone too far. Morgan acted more as an advisor to the Pepper Street boys than an enforcer, although much of his counsel consisted of trying to convince the kids of different ethnicities to stay away from one another.[24]

With his mind on sports first and troublemaking second, Jack ignored homework as much as he could. "In classroom work my will to excel wasn't there," he admitted. "I was a mediocre C."[25] In later years he would defend himself by noting that other young black men he knew—his older brother Frank, for instance—had studied hard in school, only to find that discrimination limited them to menial jobs after graduation. Whether he understood this at the time, though, is hard to say. Willa Mae only knew that by the age of 12 or 13, Jack would come home from Washington Junior High, dump his books on the nearest table, and run outside to play sports; next day he would grab the unread volumes as he headed back to school.[26] "When it came to work," his brother Mack confirmed, "he was lazy."[27]

A CLOSE-KNIT FAMILY

He could get away with these antics because he had always, to some degree, been coddled and cared for; after all, Jackie was the baby of the family, and he had never had the same household responsibilities that his siblings had had to handle. As the Robinson children grew into adulthood they remained close, living together at 121 Pepper Street with their hardworking mother and a rotating array of aunts, uncles, cousins, and friends who needed a home for a few weeks or years. However crowded the house became, Mallie turned no one away.

In 1927 they made room for Edna Sims McGriff, Mallie's mother, who migrated west to join them after her husband Wash's death that year. Jack was fascinated by his grandmother: "I remember sitting by the flickering light of an oil lantern and watching her face, which had a thousand wrinkles in it." Edna told stories about her life as a slave, the fear that so many had felt when freedom finally came, and the value of standing up for one's rights and one's dignity. Her words would stay with Jack long after her death in 1933.[28]

Edgar was a grown man by the time Jack entered junior high school. With no schooling past the sixth grade, he was helping to support the family as best he could with a series of odd jobs. Edgar was "sickly" and "mysterious" to his youngest brother, sometimes lashing out in angry rages, sometimes whizzing around town at breakneck speeds on his bicycle, and other times peacefully studying the Bible for hours on end.[29] Some believed that Edgar was mentally disabled, but he still managed to make a contribution to the family's well-being.

Jackie felt much more close to his brother Frank, whose gentleness and stalwart support had made him a kind of father figure. Frank had been a diligent student, but had the bad luck to come of age just as the Great Depression hit in 1929. When the job market tightened, Pasadena's blacks were the first to feel the squeeze. It took years for Frank to find steady work, and he too continued to live at 121 Pepper Street through Jackie's teens. "He was always there to protect me in a scrap," Robinson would say later, "even though I don't think he could knock down a fly."[30]

Willa Mae remained the "little mother" of the household and was never able to focus on developing her own sports skills. She was Jack's favorite relative, he would always say. But he suspected that she "was sort of sorry that she wasn't a boy because she liked athletics so much."[31] She played basketball, track, and soccer at Muir Technical High School, earning letters in all three sports.[32]

Mack was the sibling Jackie most admired and idolized. A gifted sprinter and broad jumper, he would sometimes take his little brother along to his high-school track meets, where the boy was awestruck by the roaring crowds. As a child, Mack had enjoyed team sports just as much as his younger brother did and had showed as much or more promise. But when a doctor doing a routine physical detected a heart murmur, Washington Junior High banned Mack from participating in its sports program. Crushed, he pleaded with Mallie to intervene. She managed to work out a deal that allowed Mack to compete in noncontact sports, in exchange for her promise not to hold the school responsible for any consequences.[33] "Noncontact sports" meant track and field, and Mack attacked them with a vengeance. He soon found that the pure competition of the events appealed to him, and he set broad-jump records while in junior high and high school.

The 1932 Olympics, held right at the Robinsons' doorstep in Los Angeles, inspired Mack to a new goal: becoming a member of the U.S. Olympic track team. To pursue this dream, Mack planned to enroll in Pasadena Junior College when he graduated from high school in June of 1935, taking advantage of the school's excellent athletic program and facilities (the football team, for instance, played its games in Pasadena's Rose Bowl), not to mention its free tuition and its fully integrated campus. Jackie watched as Mack pushed himself in his training. His fierce focus was something the boy would not forget.

Meanwhile, Jack himself was growing as an athlete. Washington Junior High had a well organized sports program, and he jumped into it with both feet, playing basketball and baseball, running track, and—his new love—leading the football team as its quarterback. He displayed "amazing skill" at the position, Mack would say years later, "calling out deceptive plays, throwing passes with accuracy and skill far beyond his age. He was tricky, too. Frequently, he would look one way and pass another."[34] He was a fast and nimble runner, with sure hands and unstoppable aggression on the field. His family always turned out for his games; Frank, in particular, never missed a chance to see him play.

But while Pasadenans of all races would cheer for Jack during games, life beyond athletics was just as painfully segregated as ever. As the members of the Pepper Street Gang grew older, their run-ins with the police became more threatening and charged. One time the boys were hauled off to the local police precinct for illegally swimming in the reservoir. The city pools were closed to them most of the time, they reasoned, so why not cool off any way they could? "I honestly thought the officials didn't think Negroes got as warm and uncomfortable as white people during the Pasadena heat,"[35] Jack complained. Some of the officers taunted the boys, calling them "niggers" and "coons" and even bringing watermelon slices to their cramped jail cell to mock them.[36]

In the face of such humiliation, only sports, and the caring interest of a few adults, kept Jack from becoming a full-scale juvenile delinquent. One of those concerned men was Carl Anderson, a young mechanic who worked near the street corner where the Pepper Street boys liked to meet. Anderson founded a black Boy Scout troop in the neighborhood when the existing group refused to integrate. He organized informal sports leagues and gathered groups of kids at his home on Friday nights to keep them off the streets and out of trouble. Anderson managed to convince the young Robinson that gang activity would sooner or later lead him into serious trouble that "would hurt my mother as well as myself," Robinson would remember.[37] It was the one message that could get through to him: disappointing his mother was simply not an option.

Jack left Washington Junior High School early in 1935. As a graduation gift, "through some miracle," Mallie managed to buy him a brand-new dress suit. After a lifetime of hand-me-downs and second-hand clothes, the sight of it brought the teenager to tears.[38] He did not always understand his mother's choices or her motives; years later, he would admit that his teenaged self thought that Mallie was nothing but a soft touch who let "parasites" get the better of her.[39] But he never doubted her love for him, and the suit showed just how well she understood her youngest child.

Right after graduation, Jack enrolled at John Muir Technical High, which Willa Mae and Mack both attended, for the spring semester. Muir was known throughout southern California for its sports program. The Terriers were a dominant force in local athletics, and in his first semester at the school, Jackie Robinson made his mark, making the baseball team as a shortstop and competing alongside Mack on the track team in the broad jump and the high jump. With Jackie at short, the Terriers went all the way to the finals in the regional baseball championship, though they lost the game to Long Beach.

In the fall, Jack went out for football and made the team, though not as a starter. He saw some action at quarterback late in the season, showing off his running and passing skills for an undefeated Muir squad. As soon as football ended, he jumped right into basketball, excelling as a guard and driving the team all season. The Terriers came within a single game of capturing the league championship that year. The end of basketball meant the beginning of baseball (as catcher this season because the team needed one) and track, and so Jack revolved through the school year, from one sport to the next. He developed his baseball skills further in a summer clinic at Brookside Park run by the baseball coach from Pasadena Junior College (PJC), John Thurman. Thurman was keeping a close eye on Jack's development, hoping he would follow his brother into PJC.

Mack was clearly the sports star of the family. He was attending PJC, though he was only a part-time student, with sports as his main focus. He quickly gained respect as the track program's "iron man," winning for PJC in the 100- and 220-yard sprints, the low hurdles, and the broad jump, and anchoring the school's sprint relay team. At PJC he would set a national junior college broad-jump record at 25 feet, 5-1/2 inches. Now established on the national level as an elite sprinter and jumper, Mack won his long-sought place on the U.S. Olympic track team in July of 1936.

Later that summer, Jack and his family huddled around their kitchen-table radio to listen to 3 A.M. broadcasts from the 1936 Olympics in Berlin, where Mack represented the United States on a track team that included Jesse Owens and Ralph Metcalfe. From tenant farming in rural Georgia to international competition in Europe within one generation was an unimaginable triumph for the Robinsons.

The 1936 Olympics would be a triumph for all Americans, in fact. The German leader, Adolf Hitler, meant these Olympic Games to display the might of Nazi Germany and the superiority of the so-called Aryan race. This was not lost on the American track team, which included black and Jewish runners. Owens was the undisputed star of the group: his four gold medals were seen as a symbol of democracy's defiance against fascism in the United States and around the world. (The team was equally aware of the irony that Owens and his black teammates would return to an America that treated them as second-class citizens or worse.)

Mack Robinson had his own success in the 1936 Games, earning a silver medal, behind Owens' gold, in the 200-meter dash. When he was left off the gold-medal-winning 400-meter relay team, however, Mack became resentful and angry. He had a successful post-Olympic tour of Europe with his teammates, even tying the world record in the 200 meters at a meet in Paris. However, this was not enough to make up for the gold medal that Mack believed he should have had.

On the team's return to New York, they were greeted not with a ticker-tape parade, but with the prospect of segregated hotels. "I just said to myself 'the hell with it' and went home," Mack said later. "But it wasn't any different in Pasadena."[40] He returned to PJC as a part-time student, keeping his amateur athletic status intact. When he went out looking for paid work, though, silver medal or no, the best Mack was offered was an overnight street-sweeping job. In defiance, or perhaps just for warmth, he would wear his leather USA Olympic team jacket as he cleaned Pasadena's streets.[41]

Watching Mack's triumphs and disappointments were formative experiences for his youngest brother. From Mack, Jack was learning that it really was possible to achieve a dream, and that once the cheering stopped, the silence could be deathly.

NOTES

1. Jackie Robinson, "Now I Know Why They Boo Me!" *Look*, January 15, 1955, pp. 22–28.

2. Robinson, "Now I Know Why They Boo Me!" pp. 22–28. It should be noted that Robinson's sister Willa Mae strongly disagreed with these assertions about the family's poverty and blamed them on "the desire of writers to foster a rags-to-riches story once Jack had become a star." See Arnold Rampersad, *Jackie Robinson: A Biography* (New York: Ballantine Books, 1998), p. 23.

3. Rampersad, *Jackie Robinson*.

4. David Falkner, *Great Time Coming* (New York: Simon and Schuster, 1995), p. 16.

5. Rampersad, *Jackie Robinson*, p. 14.

6. Jackie Robinson, *I Never Had It Made* (New York: Ecco, 1995), p. 4. One source (Falkner, *Great Time Coming*, p. 16) asserts that a telegram sent to the family "years later" informed them of Jerry's death. Another (Rampersad, *Jackie Robinson*, p. 29) holds that Jerry died in 1921.

7. Falkner, *Great Time Coming*, p. 17.

8. Jackie Robinson, *Baseball Has Done It* (Brooklyn, NY: Ig Publishing, 2005), p. 41.

9. Falkner, *Great Time Coming*.

10. Rampersad, *Jackie Robinson*, p. 23.

11. Robinson, *I Never Had It Made*, p. 6.

12. Falkner, *Great Time Coming*, p. 26.

13. Jackie Robinson as told to Ed Reid, "Jackie Robinson Tells His Own Story," *Washington Post*, August 21, 1949, p. C1.

14. Robinson, *I Never Had It Made*, p. 5.

15. Robinson, "Now I Know Why They Boo Me!" pp. 22–28.

16. Mack Robinson, "My Brother Jackie," *Ebony*, July 1957, pp. 75–82.

17. Robinson, "Jackie Robinson Tells His Own Story," *Washington Post*, August 21, 1949. Robinson later said, in his book *Baseball Has Done It* (p. 42), that he was in fourth grade at the time.

18. Falkner, *Great Time Coming*, p. 29.

19. Rampersad, *Jackie Robinson*, p. 33.

20. Robinson, *Baseball Has Done It*, p. 42.

21. Jackie Robinson, "Your Temper Can Ruin Us!" *Look*, February 22, 1955, pp. 78–87.

22. Robinson, "Your Temper Can Ruin Us!" pp. 78–87; Robinson, *I Never Had It Made*, p. 6.

23. Falkner, *Great Time Coming*, p. 31.

24. Rampersad, *Jackie Robinson*, p. 34.

25. Robinson, *Baseball Has Done It*, pp. 43–44.

26. Rampersad, *Jackie Robinson*, p. 28.

27. Robinson, "My Brother Jackie," pp. 75–82

28. Jackie Robinson as told to Ed Reid, "Being an Athlete Gets Robinson Out of a Jam," *Washington Post*, August 22, 1949, pp. 8–9; Rampersad, *Jackie Robinson*, p. 108.

29. Robinson, "Jackie Robinson Tells His Own Story," *Washington Post*, August 21, 1949.

30. Robinson, "Jackie Robinson Tells His Own Story," *Washington Post*, August 21, 1949.

31. Robinson, "Jackie Robinson Tells His Own Story," *Washington Post*, August 21, 1949.

32. Glenn Stout and Dick Johnson, *Jackie Robinson: Between the Baselines* (San Francisco: Woodford Press, 1997), p. 17.

33. Falkner, *Great Time Coming*, p. 35.

34. Robinson, "My Brother Jackie," July 1957.

35. Robinson, "Jackie Robinson Tells His Own Story," *Washington Post*, August 21, 1949.

36. Falkner, *Great Time Coming*.

37. Robinson, *I Never Had It Made*, p. 7.

38. Jackie Robinson as told to Ed Reid, "Robinson Never Forgets Mother's Advice," *Washington Post*, August 23, 1949, pp. 12–13.

39. Robinson, *I Never Had It Made*, p. 267.

40. Falkner, *Great Time Coming*, p. 38.

41. Rampersad, *Jackie Robinson*.

Chapter 2

COLLEGE MAN, 1936–1941

Robinson's last few months at Muir Technical High School were all about football. He drove the team to victory after victory with an intense running game that had him using his versatile speed and agility in every situation. He played safety on defense, he could pass and run from tailback on offense, and his speed made him the team's best punt returner.

His sports achievements helped to give him a self-assured, almost cocky attitude. It was a front, though, a mask he wore to keep outsiders at arm's length. He did not often reach outside his comfortable circle to make new friends. Within this small group of neighborhood teens, he was seen as quiet and shy, if often mischievously "devilish." Friends would remember him tossing firecrackers in the street, or jostling pals to make them drop their popcorn at the movies. "He was just a devilish guy," one schoolmate would recall. "He was definitely not a bully... everything was a lot of fun to Jack."[1]

He didn't even date, partly because of this cautious shyness, and partly, Robinson later admitted, because of "the knowledge that we were very poor."[2] The money from the odd jobs he did—selling hot dogs at Rose Bowl events, delivering newspapers, shining shoes, running errands—went to help the family. There wasn't much left over to spend on girls.

His final football game for Muir was the conference championship of 1936, played against Glendale High in the storied Rose Bowl. As the team's mainstay, Robinson was so feared that the Glendale players decided to get him out of the game early with a deliberate hit just after the opening kickoff. Robinson, taken completely off guard, was knocked to the ground and sidelined with two broken ribs. His tackler was white. "It was a bigot's reminder that he intended to drive me off the gridiron, single-handed," Robinson believed.[3] Without him on the field, Muir lost the game.

PASADENA JUNIOR COLLEGE

Completing high school at the end of January, Robinson followed his brother Mack into Pasadena Junior College (PJC). That spring he made the baseball team at shortstop. He was an eye-catching fielder and a patient hitter who quickly took the leadoff spot in the lineup. The freshman's real genius, though, was on the basepaths: A constant threat to steal, he drove opposing pitchers to distraction. In one game Robinson stole second base, then third and home, to create a run for the Bulldogs out of a single hit. The local newspaper ran his photograph with its account of the contest. When PJC went on a 14-game winning streak that April, Robinson was given much of the credit.

At the same time he ran with the PJC track team, to which Mack had returned after his Olympic experience. The younger Robinson consistently placed second to his brother, but this was one rival he did not mind losing to; he treasured the chance to spend time with Mack, training and traveling with him and the team. For his part, Mack seemed to thrive on the challenge of competing with his kid brother, and he had one of the most successful seasons of his junior college career. It led to a scholarship offer from the University of Oregon, which Mack accepted the next spring.

At PJC, Robinson would say later, "I lost most of the shyness that had always made my early life miserable."[4] That first semester he got to know Jack Gordon, who had been a football rival in junior high and high school. Now he became a teammate and close friend. Robinson also began going out with his first steady girlfriend—Elizabeth "Bessie" Renfro, a girl from the neighborhood who had had her eye on him since junior high.[5] Gordon was going out with a girl who was a close friend of Bessie's, and soon the two couples were double dating.

When classes ended for the summer, Robinson played shortstop for a team in a local semi-pro Owl League, a softball-baseball hybrid that was popular in California. Here Robinson sharpened his baserunning still further, stealing bases with abandon and making his signature move—the steal of home—in game after game. As local sportswriter Rube Samuelson put it, "That isn't stealing. It's grand larceny."[6]

That summer, whenever traveling teams of Negro League ballplayers came through the area on their irregular barnstorming tours, Robinson would join with other Pasadenans to compete against them. One time the pros, down a few players, asked him and a friend to play on their side, promising them $20 each for their trouble. Afterward, though, the man who was supposed to pay them was nowhere to be found. "I decided then and there that Negro baseball was not for me," Robinson said.[7]

As his first fall semester at Pasadena Junior College began, Robinson went out for the football team and immediately "ran into the color problem in sports," as he put it.[8] A new head coach, Tom Mallory, had arrived from Oklahoma City, Oklahoma, bringing along a contingent of players from his former whites-only school. The Oklahoma men had never competed with or against blacks. When Robinson made the team as starting quarterback, along with his friend Ray Bartlett and another black student, the transplants at first refused to take the field for an integrated practice.

Coach Mallory's intervention got the white players to grudgingly accept the blacks as teammates, but Robinson and Bartlett "wanted a winning team, twenty-five guys united to win." That would take more time.[9]

When the PJC squad went out for its first scrimmage, even the most bigoted teammate had to respect Robinson's skills. "Time and again Robinson broke loose from the defense with his spectacular style of running," wrote a reporter for the school newspaper.[10] Then, in the team's second formal practice session, Robinson twisted his right ankle. It was painful, but it didn't seem debilitating; the coaches taped it up and Robinson kept playing. After another day or so, as the pain worsened, he had to admit that this was more than just a sprain. Jack Gordon took his friend to a hospital emergency room, where an x-ray revealed a broken ankle. Robinson spent the first four games of PJC's season on the bench. The Bulldogs lost them all.

He was back in action for the fifth game, on the road against Phoenix Junior College. Segregated Phoenix, Arizona would not house the team in one hotel, and the black players refused the rooms offered them. "I think we just sat up and talked in the lobby area and maybe we slept sitting up in chairs," Ray Bartlett remembered.[11] Despite this, Robinson was itching to get into the game. He came in as a substitute and promptly scored a touchdown in the Bulldogs' first victory of the season. They would not lose again in 1937, or in 1938 either for that matter: this was the first win of what would become a 16-game winning streak, driven by the spectacular play of Jackie Robinson. In one game, playing safety, he ran an 80-yard punt return for a touchdown; in another, as quarterback, he both ran and passed brilliantly. His tricky running style, incorporating sudden stops, nimble sidesteps, and blazing accelerations, kept opponents confused and off-balance. His team-first attitude, meanwhile, won over the Oklahomans and the other white players by the end of the season. As quarterback, Robinson made sure to spread his passes, and thus the scoring and the glory, around to everyone on the field. In return, his teammates blocked for him fiercely. The prejudice that had divided the men disappeared, and the team finally came together.

When the football season ended in December, Robinson went out for PJC's basketball team. Basketball was an afterthought at Pasadena compared to the football program, but Robinson played both sports with equal passion. The Bulldogs finished the season third in their conference; Robinson was one point behind the leading scorer in the division, despite his and his teammates' belief that a suspiciously large number of calls made by the all-white referees went against the integrated PJC squad. At one of their home games, against Long Beach on January 22, race-related tensions resulted in a near riot. It started at the final whistle, when a white Long Beach guard who had been taunting Robinson throughout the game took a swipe at him. Robinson struck back, and at least 50 players, coaches, and fans jumped into the subsequent melee.

Incidents like this one began to give Robinson a reputation as a hothead. He was not willing to stay silent in the face of racist insults, as so many blacks felt they must do simply to survive in a bigoted society. And when unreasonably challenged by a police officer—as happened so often to a young African American man, then and now—Robinson "just wouldn't back down," as Bartlett put it. "He was just stubborn."[12]

A few days after the basketball brawl, Robinson's belligerent image was sealed when he was arrested and spent a night in the city jail. The incident itself was almost laughably minor: walking home one night, a friend of Robinson's began to sing a song that a white police officer took as an insult. That led to an argument, which quickly became an arrest. A January 25 hearing resulted in a 10-day jail sentence. Since this was Robinson's first offense—and perhaps also because of his athletic fame—the judge suspended the jail time, on the condition that he avoid another arrest for two years.

All in all it was a difficult month for Robinson. There was one bright spot: the arrival of Karl Downs, a vibrant young minister, at Scott United Methodist church. Downs, just 25 years old, was an athlete who had competed in basketball and softball while growing up in Texas. When he chose to follow his father into the ministry, he was determined to reach out to other young African Americans. He saw in them a way to revitalize the faith community, and he understood their need for respect and dignity in a deeply prejudiced world. Downs was not afraid of controversy; two years earlier he had published an article calling on black students to stand up against social injustices. He came to Pasadena full of plans for a youth center, athletic programs, dances, libraries, radio programs, interracial social events, and more, all designed to spark the enthusiasm of teens and young adults.[13]

To achieve these dreams—which he did within his first few years at Scott—Downs had to win over the young people he saw as leaders. Jack Robinson, whose sense of faith and religious commitment had flagged in his late teens, was one of the first Downs got to know. He quickly charmed the young man. "Karl Downs had the ability to communicate with you spiritually, and at the same time he was fun to be with," Robinson said.[14] Soon Robinson and many other members of the old Pepper Street Gang stopped hanging out on the streets and poured their energy into Downs's projects.

Once the PJC basketball season ended, Robinson went immediately on to baseball and track. This semester, with Mack away at the University of Oregon, Jack came into his own on the track team. At a meet in Pomona on May 7, he broke his big brother's national junior college broad jump record with a leap of 25 feet 6-½ inches. But his schedule gave him no time to bask in the achievement; the baseball Bulldogs were at that moment taking the field in Glendale, 40 miles away. "Jack [Gordon] drove me to Glendale while I changed into my baseball uniform in the car," Robinson said. "The ball game was in the fourth inning. I got two hits before it was over."[15] The baseball team went on to win the divisional title that season, led by Robinson's .417 batting average and 25 steals. Robinson even pitched the team to a 12–1 victory in one game. When the White Sox came to the area for spring training that March and played an exhibition game against a team of young Pasadenans, Robinson put his dizzying baserunning and crisp fielding on display. "Geez," said White Sox manager Jimmy Dykes, "if that kid was white I'd sign him right now."[16]

In July, PJC sent Robinson to the National Amateur Athletic Association's annual track meet, held in Buffalo, New York. Mack was there, too, representing Oregon. Jack placed third in the broad jump; Mack won the 200-meter race. But it was the last competition the two would share. Mack, who had married and would soon become a father, never returned to the University of Oregon. Instead, he went home to Pasadena and his street-sweeping job. "I had to take whatever I could get," he had decided.[17]

The rest of Jack's summer was spent outdoors as usual, playing golf, tennis, and—more and more seriously—baseball. His spectacular play at shortstop and on the basepaths began to attract unheard-of crowds to his team's Owl League games: 5,000 turned out for a contest that August in Brookside Park.

Still, football was the sport that Robinson liked best. The PJC team, almost intact from the season before, went undefeated in 1938 as Robinson's broken-field running—aided by the blocking of his now-loyal Oklahoman teammates—carried them to eleven straight wins.

As had been the case during his summertime ballgames, people turned out in droves to witness Robinson's feats on the field. A game against Compton in the Rose Bowl drew 40,000 fans, a junior college record at the time. The crowds were rewarded by Robinson's spectacular brand of football in game after game. In a contest with Santa Ana, Robinson was the prime mover behind every one of Pasadena's touchdowns. Against Los Angeles, he freed himself from the clutches of four separate defenders to score. He ran for touchdowns on 75-yard, 85-yard, and even 104-yard carries.

As his two years at junior college drew to a close, Robinson's outstanding play that season made him a hot commodity for four-year colleges up and down the West Coast. That fall there was a recruiting rush on the young man. In an era of little regulation within college sports, he heard several unusual proposals. One school offered him a set of tires for his car as an inducement; another promised apartments close to campus for himself, his mother, and his girlfriend. Odder still was the offer from an alumnus of segregated Stanford University, which would not allow Robinson to enroll under any circumstances. The Stanford fan pledged to pay Robinson's expenses at any college he might choose to attend—as long as that school did not play in Stanford's conference.

UCLA

When it was time to make a decision, Robinson's brother Frank took a large part in it. Frank had been Jack's most loyal fan, attending game after game throughout his high school and junior college sports career. Married now, with two small children, he was the brother Jack most looked to for emotional support. Jack wanted to remain close to Frank and the rest of the family, so he was uninterested in offers from faraway schools like the University of Oregon.[18] Instead, he looked at colleges closer to home.

The standout, in Frank's mind, was the University of California at Los Angeles (UCLA). UCLA was a new school in California's state university system, and a relatively comfortable one for black students. Its football team was strong and featured black players in key roles, including receiver Woody Strode and halfback Kenny Washington; the 1938 season ended with the Bruins' first-ever bowl game appearance.[19] The school would be financially reasonable, too: its location meant that Robinson could continue to live at home in Pasadena, and since tuition was free for state residents, he would have to pay only a nominal administrative fee each year.[20]

While Robinson was pondering his decision, UCLA announced the signing of Edwin C. "Babe" Horrell as its new football coach. Horrell was a Pasadenan who had been a legendary PJC athlete. For Robinson, it seems to have confirmed that UCLA was meant for him. Two weeks later, a local newspaper reported that the university would be his top choice.[21] Horrell, who called Robinson "one of the greatest open-field runners I have ever seen," was excited to have him.[22]

Robinson began attending classes at a UCLA extension program in February of 1939. He focused his attention firmly on academics that spring semester, taking English, French, physiology, physical education, algebra, and geometry to catch up to his new classmates at the university. And he announced plans to devote himself to only two varsity sports, football and track, once he enrolled at UCLA. He planned to devote the extra time to his training for the 1940 Olympic track-and-field team.[23]

He couldn't bear to stay completely away from athletic competition, though. That spring he played basketball in a statewide league for black fraternity members, and in early July, Robinson competed in the championship tournament of the Western Federation of Tennis Clubs, which offered African Americans a chance to play this largely segregated sport. As in every other sport he tried, Robinson dominated his matches with a tough and aggressive playing style that was especially startling in what was then a relatively staid game. He easily won the men's singles and doubles crowns. Reporters made a point to note that Robinson, who only played tennis in the summer as a sideline, beat players who devoted themselves to the sport year-round.[24]

Days later, Robinson was relaxing at a friend's house when he got word that Frank had been hurt in a traffic accident. His brother had been riding his motorcycle and had collided with a car on a busy street not far from home. Jack rushed to Huntington Memorial Hospital to find that the injuries had been severe. Frank's skull had been fractured, he had broken several ribs and a leg, and he had suffered terrible internal injuries. As Mallie, Jack, and other family members gathered around Frank's hospital bed, it was clear that he was in excruciating pain. In despair, Jack rushed home to Pepper Street, sobbing. There was nothing that he, or Frank's doctors, could do. Within hours, Frank was dead.

Frank's loss was emotionally devastating, and it would reverberate in his brother's life for years to come. That summer, though, Jack dealt with the pain by pouring all his efforts into athletics, translating his feelings into fierceness on the field. He played semi-pro baseball with the Pasadena Sox, a mixed-race team sponsored by the Chicago White Sox. They won the league championship in a game in which Robinson scored two runs, stole four bases, and sparkled defensively. One newspaper account pointed out how comfortably the members of the Pasadena Sox played together, despite the widespread notion that black and whites could never get along as teammates. According to the reporter, the team's success was "the biggest argument for the participation of the Negro in major league baseball."[25]

In fact, controversy over the "color line" in professional baseball had been bubbling for several years, though perhaps not in a way that would have been known to the 20-year-old Jackie Robinson. The rule barring blacks from Major League Baseball was an unwritten one: the game's longtime commissioner, Judge Kenesaw Mountain Landis, could honestly state that there was "no rule, formal or informal, or any understanding— unwritten, subterranean, or sub-anything—against the hiring of Negro players by the teams of organized ball."[26] It was collusion by the teams' owners that kept dark-skinned players out. Black ballplayers had their own Negro Leagues, the owners reasoned; segregation was the law in much of America. There was the risk of trouble in their teams' clubhouses, or among fans in the stands, if a black ballplayer was signed. Besides, many major- and minor-league teams within "organized baseball" made money from the existing Negro League teams, which used their fields and stadiums whenever the white teams were on the road. The status quo was working very well for them.

The status quo was undeniably unfair, though, and all through the 1930s that case was being made more and more insistently in black newspapers like the *Pittsburgh Courier* and communist newspapers like the *Daily Worker*. That the Chicago White Sox would create a mixed-race exhibition team like the Pasadena Sox, thus exposing the organization's scouts, players, and prospects to talented black athletes, was one sign that attitudes within Major League Baseball were slowly—very slowly— beginning to change.

That change seemed impossibly far away to Jackie Robinson, however, and the everyday injustices he had to confront, combined with his grief over Frank's sudden death, became increasingly difficult to take. Tensions exploded on September 5, just before Robinson was set to formally en- roll at UCLA. He was driving his old heap of a car, packed with friends and teammates, home from a pickup ballgame. Robinson stopped to let someone out, angering the white driver of the car behind him. The man "leaned out of the car and cussed us out, but good," Robinson recalled, and both cars emptied. A crowd gathered as the argument continued.[27]

The angry driver began to back down when he noticed he had become surrounded by so many black faces, but by then the incident had drawn the attention of a passing motorcycle cop. Rather than calm things down, the white police officer belligerently drove his machine into the crowd and attempted to arrest several of the black men in the center of the circle. One after another, they slipped away from him into the crowd—all but one. Only Jack Robinson stood his ground, as Ray Bartlett remembered, "right in the middle of it, as usual."[28]

Frustrated and angry, the police officer "pulled out his revolver and began waving it around, yelling and bellowing," Robinson wrote later. "I found myself up against the side of my car with a gun barrel pressed unsteadily into the pit of my stomach. I was scared to death."[29]

Robinson, the only person taken into custody, was charged with hindering traffic, resisting arrest, and suspicion of robbery. He spent the night in jail without even a chance to make a phone call. Next morning, when he was finally allowed to use the phone, he reached out to John Thurman, his baseball coach at PJC. Thurman understood immediately that the young man needed help, and fast. Robinson was still on probation from that January 1938 arrest, and nothing could be allowed to get in the way of his soon-to-begin football season at UCLA.

While Thurman began making a chain of phone calls of his own, Robinson was brought before a judge to be arraigned. He pleaded not guilty to the traffic and resistance charges (he had been cleared of the robbery overnight) and put up $25 bail.

In the end, "I got out of that trouble because I was an athlete," Robinson said.[30] Between Babe Horrell's contacts within Pasadena and the influence of UCLA, a prominent attorney was found who could convince a sympathetic judge that, as the lawyer's request put it, "the Negro player be not disturbed during the football season."[31] They worked out a deal, without Robinson's involvement, to change his plea to guilty, forfeit his bail money, and fine him $50. The university took care of all the expenses, and Robinson never even had to show up in court.

The whole situation, though, upset Robinson deeply. First of all, the guilty plea offended his sense of justice: he had done nothing wrong. He was bothered that his status as a star athlete had gotten him out of the jam; the outcome would have been very different had he been a young black man without those connections. Worst of all, he knew that the incident would give him an undeserved image as a thug. The press got hold of the story quickly, "and didn't the newspapers come out with a big blast and paint it up pretty," he noted indignantly. "The whole deal gave me a bad name at UCLA ... this thing followed me all over and it was pretty hard to shake off."[32]

With the court case still unfolding, Robinson enrolled at UCLA and began to settle into his new routine there. Having decided to major in physical education, with the idea of becoming a coach or teacher once he completed school, he registered for classes in history, education, and geology, as well as in his major. He commuted to campus in his car or by bus and socialized mainly within the small community of perhaps 50 black students who gathered regularly in a particular area in Kerckhoff Hall, the student union. Among them was his old friend Ray Bartlett. Robinson immediately joined the football team and began to benefit from its major perk: the training table. This was the food that the team provided for its players to keep them well-nourished during the season. "That was our main meal," Bartlett said. "We didn't have any money in our pockets and we looked forward to [the] training table because they fed us very well, steaks and all the good heavy meat and potatoes stuff."[33]

The Bruins built on the success of their previous season as they welcomed Robinson onto the team. He seemed to provide the missing piece that the team needed: they went undefeated, with six wins and four ties, in 1939. Coach Horrell's plan was to use Robinson, playing halfback, mainly as a decoy to clear the way for the team's star runner, the senior Kenny Washington. It worked; wherever Robinson went on the field, he would draw two or three defenders along with him, freeing Washington to run and to score. Washington led all of college football in total yards, earning him all-American honors that season.

When Robinson did get the chance to run the ball himself, he was nearly unstoppable. In only 42 opportunities, he averaged 11.4 yards per carry and made some spectacularly memorable plays.

The Bruins' first game of the season was an upset victory over the highly ranked Texas Christian University, whose players were left agog at Washington's speed and Robinson's agility. The next week, against the University of Washington, Robinson rallied the team with a dazzling 65-yard punt return, and the Bruins took that game, too. They battled Stanford to a tie on a last-minute interception by Robinson and his subsequent 55-yard run deep into their opponents' territory.[34]

Their final game of 1939 pitted the Bruins against the University of Southern California (USC), their greatest rival, for the Pacific Coast Conference championship. The winner would secure a place in the annual Rose Bowl game. The two teams met in the massive Los Angeles Coliseum, which was packed with 103,352 delirious fans, and in a peerless defensive display ended the game in a scoreless tie. USC, with one fewer tied game that season, took the conference crown.

After the loss, despite a terrific tackle and a glittering season, Robinson was inconsolable. He ran the locker-room shower so no one would hear him weep. A "good-enough" year could not possibly satisfy his intense drive to win.

While the football team's success made Robinson well known on campus, it did not make him popular. He was as reserved as ever, though some classmates would describe him as withdrawn, sullen, or unfriendly rather than shy. Others detected a rage within him, an anger that could flash from his eyes with little provocation. Few if any of these new classmates would have connected Robinson's demeanor with his frustration over the arrest and its aftermath, or with his grief over Frank's shattering death.

For his part, Robinson believed that college was little more than an "academic and athletic dream world."[35] He had seen tragedy and injustice up close, and Mack's experience—from Olympian and college star to street sweeper in just a few years—convinced him that athletic success, however thrilling, would never translate into success elsewhere. He enjoyed his onfield victories but did not get swept up in them.

Those who got to know Robinson found him to be likable and intelligent, and by all accounts he performed his part-time jobs—as a janitor at Kerckhoff Hall and a clerk at an off-campus bookstore—dependably and well. The bookstore owners, Bob and Blanche Campbell, became especially close to Robinson; they helped him finance a newer, more reliable car, and they invited Mallie to attend the Bruins' annual celebratory dinner with them.

These new friends knew that the money from his part-time jobs went mainly to help support the extended Robinson family, which now lived in two adjacent houses on Pepper Street and included Frank's widow and her children. And they knew of the continuing influence of Karl Downs in the young man's life. "Reverend Downs watched me play football on Saturdays and then made sure that I taught my Sunday-school class the following morning," Robinson would write later.[36] The pillars of his life—family and faith—remained constant for him.

Robinson had not planned to play varsity basketball for UCLA, much to the chagrin of the coach, Wilbur Johns, who had followed his Pasadena basketball career and badly wanted him for the team. But war in Europe made Robinson rethink his plans. Nazi Germany had invaded Poland that September, launching the conflict that would become World War II. On November 30, 1939, when the war expanded with the Soviet Union's invasion of Finland, the 1940 Olympic Games were canceled. That wiped out Robinson's Olympic dream, along with his wish to limit his athletic efforts to football and track. He went out for the basketball team as soon as the football season ended and immediately won a spot on a squad that had lost its last 28 consecutive games. Coach Johns had gotten his wish.

There was a problem, though: Johns favored a slow and deliberate set-up style of offense, while Robinson's speed and agility made him a better match for a fast-break approach. The team did poorly in its first two games of the season; Robinson, who so hated to lose, was infuriated. His irritation led to acts of open defiance, such as skipped practices, that brought matters to a head. Johns called him into his office and the two had it out. From then on, Robinson's behavior toward his coach became more cooperative—and the team began to use the fast break on the court.

Johns and Robinson began a relationship marked by mutual respect that would endure long past their days at UCLA together. The Bruins ended their losing streak at 31 games, with Robinson leading the charge. He averaged 12 points per game (at a time when team scores for entire games rarely rose far above 30), and he shot a conference-high 148 points on the season. It was his team spirit, though, that most impressed his coach. If victory required it, Robinson would often ignore a scoring opportunity to slow the game and preserve a Bruins lead. "He might have been the greatest of all basketball players" if he hadn't focused more firmly on football or ultimately baseball, Johns believed. "His timing was perfect. His rhythm was unmatched." What's more, "he always placed the welfare of the team above his chance for greater stardom."[37]

Robinson leaped right into UCLA baseball as soon as he could, joining Ray Bartlett and the rest of the team for the first game of the season with little chance to train with them. His first game was a gem: Robinson got four hits and stole four bases, including a steal of home that had already become his signature move. That, though, was his best performance for the Bruins. He had only two more hits in the rest of the short 11-game season and ended up with an .097 batting average. His defensive play at shortstop was inspired at times, but he also racked up 10 errors.

After baseball, it was on to the track team, which he was not permitted to join at first because of the coach's suspicions about his commitment. When Robinson casually landed a 23-foot broad jump in an informal practice, the coach thought better of that decision. That season Robinson set a Pacific Coast Conference record with a broad jump of 25 feet, and he went on to win the 1940 NCAA broad jump championship.[38]

During the summer, for the first time in years, Robinson did not join one of Brookside Park's semi-pro baseball teams. He had earned four varsity letters in the past school year; perhaps he felt he deserved a rest. Instead, he took a well-paying job in the props department at the Warner Brothers movie studio, which was arranged through yet another UCLA athletics booster.

Robinson returned to campus for his senior year as the star of the football team, now that Washington and Woody Strode had graduated. Unfortunately, neither of them had been replaced by players of similar talent. That made Robinson the star of a distinctly less skilled team, without anyone to anchor the offensive line, as he had for Washington. The Bruins of 1940 had just one victory and nine losses, though Robinson's own statistics were strong. He was second in his conference in total offense, with 440 yards rushing and 435 yards passing, and he set a national record for punt returns with 21 yards per return.

For the first time, though, sports were overshadowed by something else in Robinson's life. That semester a new student arrived on campus. Rachel Isum was a freshman, a serious straight-A scholar who planned to study nursing. She had grown up in south Los Angeles in a small, tight-knit family. Her mother, Zellee, ran her own catering business. Her father, Charles, had been forced to retire from his bookbinding career when he became homebound with a heart condition, the long-delayed result of a mustard gas attack he suffered during his service in World War I. Zellee and Charles had given Rachel and her two brothers a firm and secure foundation from which she was determined to earn a college degree and make a difference in the world.

It didn't take long for Robinson to notice the pretty 17-year-old with the studious habits, but he was too shy to introduce himself to her. Finally, Ray Bartlett, who had always been more comfortable with members of the opposite sex, made the formal introductions. "I remember the awkwardness of the moment," Rachel said years later. "What I liked about Jack was his smile, and the kind of confident air about him, without being cocky in person."[39]

Robinson, who was still casually dating Bessie Renfro from Pasadena, was taken with Rachel. Her innate kindness was balanced by forthright honesty, characteristics that he found both attractive and worthy of respect. They soon found themselves going out of their way to run into one another on campus—loitering in the parking lot or waiting in Kerckhoff Hall in hopes that the other would come along. These "chance" meetings led to long talks, and the two were soon considered a couple. Their status was sealed when Robinson asked Rachel, not Bessie, to attend UCLA's homecoming dance with him on November 2.

The two had much in common, in particular their strong ties to family, and it wasn't long before each of them took the other home to meet the folks. Charles, ever protective of his only daughter, was wary. But Zellee liked Rachel's new suitor immediately. He was a "clean-cut, well-mannered Christian boy," she would say, and in the Isum household Zellee had the last word.[40] Besides, Robinson didn't drink, he didn't smoke, and he insisted on being at home in bed by midnight every night, since he always considered himself to be "in training" for one sport or another. This notion "definitely got in the way of a lot of fun," as Rachel noted, but it was reassuring for her parents.[41] Rachel, in turn, was warmly welcomed by the Robinsons. As their romance blossomed, it was with the blessing of both their families.

At the same time, though, Robinson was beginning to doubt the wisdom of continuing his college career. Professional sports were closed to him—none of the major leagues, in football, basketball, or baseball, were integrated at this point. If he were to get a job as a coach or an athletic director, he thought, the formality of a university degree would not be important. He also felt that it was time for him to help contribute more extensively to the family finances.[42] The idea of quitting school remained at the back of his mind as he played through another basketball season at UCLA. Once again, he excelled; he led the conference in scoring, with 133 points for the season. Now more than ever, though, he was a target for opposing teams, who roughed him up continually.

When the basketball season ended, he made his decision. Robinson had received a job offer from the National Youth Administration, a government program that was part of President Franklin Roosevelt's New Deal. He would not play baseball or run track for UCLA in 1941. He would not complete the classes he had begun that spring semester. Despite the entreaties of his mother, Rev. Downs, his coaches, and Rachel, on March 3 Robinson arranged his "honorable dismissal" from UCLA. That afternoon, he left college behind and began to make his way in the world.

NOTES

1. Arnold Rampersad, *Jackie Robinson: A Biography* (New York: Ballantine Books, 1998), p. 44.

2. Jackie Robinson as told to Ed Reid, "Jackie Overcomes Girl Fright," *Washington Post*, August 24, 1949, p. 13.

3. Jackie Robinson, *Baseball Has Done It* (Brooklyn, NY: Ig Publishing, 2005), pp. 44–45; David Falkner, *Great Time Coming* (New York: Simon & Schuster, 1995.

4. Jackie Robinson as told to Ed Reid, "Being an Athlete Gets Robinson Out of a Jam," *Washington Post,* August 22, 1949, p. 8.

5. Robinson, "Jackie Overcomes Girl Fright," *Washington Post*, August 24, 1949, p. 13.

6. *Pasadena Post*, July 10, 1937. Cited in Rampersad, *Jackie Robinson*, p. 44.

7. Jackie Robinson, "Your Temper Can Ruin Us!" *Look*, February 22, 1955, pp. 78–87.

8. Robinson, "Your Temper Can Ruin Us!" pp. 78–87.

9. Robinson, *Baseball Has Done It*, p. 45.

10. *Pasadena Junior College Chronicle*, September 14, 1937. Cited in Rampersad, *Jackie Robinson*, p. 45.

11. Falkner, *Great Time Coming*, p. 45.

12. Rampersad, *Jackie Robinson*, p. 65.

13. Rampersad, *Jackie Robinson*, pp. 52–53.

14. Jackie Robinson, *I Never Had It Made* (New York: Ecco, 1995), pp. 8–9.

15. Robinson, "Your Temper Can Ruin Us!" pp. 78–87.

16. *Los Angeles Times*, April 4, 1977. Cited in Rampersad, *Jackie Robinson*, p. 55.

17. *Pasadena Star-News*, April 7, 1987. Cited in Rampersad, *Jackie Robinson*, p. 56.

18. Robinson, *I Never Had It Made*, p. 10.

19. Rampersad, *Jackie Robinson*.

20. Rampersad, *Jackie Robinson*.

21. Rampersad, *Jackie Robinson*.

22. *California Daily Bruin*, February 16, 1939. Cited in Rampersad, *Jackie Robinson*, p. 62.

23. Rampersad, *Jackie Robinson*, pp. 62–63.

24. Rampersad, *Jackie Robinson*, p. 63.

25. *California Eagle*, August 17, 1939. Cited in Rampersad, *Jackie Robinson*, p. 64.

26. Geoffrey C. Ward and Ken Burns, *Baseball: An Illustrated History* (New York: Alfred A. Knopf, 1994), p. 282.

27. Jackie Robinson as told to Ed Reid, "Jackie Robinson Tells His Own Story," *Washington Post*, August 21, 1949, p. C1.

28. Rampersad, *Jackie Robinson*, p. 65.

29. Robinson, "Jackie Robinson Tells His Own Story," *Washington Post*, August 21, 1949, p. C1.

30. Robinson, "Being an Athlete Gets Robinson Out of a Jam," *Washington Post*, August 22, 1949, p. 8.

31. *Pasadena Star-News*, October 18, 1939. Cited in Rampersad, *Jackie Robinson*, p. 66.

32. Robinson, "Being an Athlete Gets Robinson Out of a Jam," *Washington Post*, August 22, 1949, p. 8.

33. Falkner, *Great Time Coming*, p. 51.

34. Rampersad, *Jackie Robinson*, p. 70.

35. Robinson, *I Never Had It Made*, p. 11.

36. Robinson, *Baseball Has Done It*, p. 42.

37. Arthur Mann, *The Jackie Robinson Story* (New York: Grosset and Dunlap, 1951), p. 59.

38. Jules Tygiel, *Baseball's Great Experiment* (New York: Oxford University Press, 1997), p. 60.

39. Rampersad, *Jackie Robinson*, p. 78.

40. Sharon Robinson, *Stealing Home* (New York: HarperPerennial, 1997), p. 39.

41. Rampersad, *Jackie Robinson*, p. 81.

42. Robinson, *I Never Had It Made*, p. 11.

Chapter 3

THE BATTLE OF CAMP
HOOD, 1941–1944

Robinson reported to his new job in April. It took him 200 miles north of home to a job-training camp in Atascadero, California. The National Youth Administration (NYA), founded in 1935, was meant to help out-of-work young people in the depths of the Great Depression. This camp, and others like it, took in teenagers up to the age of 18 and taught them a trade. Robinson was hired as assistant athletic director, charged with keeping the teens occupied with sports and other activities in their off hours. The pay was $150 a month.

Before his departure, though, he helped Rachel get through the shock of her father's death in early March. Charles Isum had had many medical scares as a result of his weak heart, but his death was unexpected. Rachel, who had been responsible for much of his care, was devastated, and she turned to Jack for comfort. The protectiveness he felt for her in her grief took him by surprise, and he realized that he was deeply in love with her.[1] When he left for Atascadero, they were informally engaged to be married—with the understanding that Rachel would complete her college studies first.

The NYA camp took some getting used to. Suddenly, the 22-year-old Robinson, not too far removed from juvenile delinquency himself, was in a position of authority over 100 or so underprivileged teens, most of them white. He set to work leading the kids though a physical fitness program that included regular calisthenics, then organizing camp teams to play baseball and football. He never held himself aloof from his charges; in fact, he wrote, "the biggest kid of all, come recreation time, was yours truly, Jackie Robinson." Doing this work that he "loved and appreciated" confirmed for him that a coaching career of some kind would be his future path.[2]

During the summer, however, the United States government began to phase out the NYA programs and close down its camps. The war in Europe was escalating, and it seemed that the nation would soon enter the conflict. The Atascadero camp was turned over to the U.S. Army as a processing and training center for draftees, and Robinson was looking for work again.

A FUTURE IN FOOTBALL?

In August he traveled to Chicago at the invitation of the *Chicago Tribune* to participate in a college-versus-NFL charity game. The newspaper had polled its readers to decide which college players to invite, and Robinson had received more than 700,000 votes. It was an all-expenses-paid, three-week experience that helped to seal Robinson's national reputation. The collegians lost the game, but according to one of the professional players, "The only time we worried was when that guy Robinson was on the field."[3]

The Chicago game, along with Robinson's local reputation, led to an offer from the Los Angeles Bulldogs, a Pacific Coast Professional Football League team for which he played in September. That appearance in turn garnered a better-paying offer from the Honolulu Bears, a semi-professional football club in Hawaii. The deal included an upfront payment, a fee for each game in which he appeared, and a construction job associated with the Pearl Harbor naval base. The job was a big inducement, not only for the additional money it would bring in, but also because it was related to national defense and would allow Robinson to avoid the military draft.

The Bears made the most of their new acquisition, advertising Robinson as "the sensational All-American halfback" and the team's star.[4] He did have some great on-field performances, but the rest of the team's play was spotty. When he aggravated his old ankle injury and had to sit out a few games, the Bears' offense collapsed. They wrapped up their short season on December 3, and Robinson decided to head back home. He boarded a ship for California on December 5.

Two days later, he and the rest of the ship's passengers were startled to learn that Pearl Harbor, the naval base they had just left behind, was under attack by Japan. The bombing occurred without warning that morning, Sunday, December 7; 19 U.S. Navy ships had been destroyed or damaged, killing more than 2,000 servicemen. The United States was at war.

Robinson returned to a Los Angeles, and a nation, transformed. The war effort was all-consuming. Workers were needed everywhere—to help build ships, rivet warplanes, manufacture guns and ammunition—and once-rigid racial barriers began to crumble. Robinson quickly landed a $100-a-week job as a truck driver at Lockheed Aircraft, which had previously been an all-white employer. He moved back into the family home at Pepper Street, glad to be making a contribution to his mother's finances, and he saw Rachel as frequently as he could. As a young and healthy man, he knew that the military would soon call on him.

CALLED UP

And soon they did. Although Robinson had registered for the draft a year before claiming to be his mother's sole support and therefore not eligible to enlist, classifications like these were being rethought now that war was declared. He received his draft notice at the end of March 1942 and was ordered to report for induction into the U.S. Army on April 3.

Meanwhile, Robinson made headlines once again when he and Nate Moreland, a Pasadenan who played with the Negro Leagues' Baltimore Elite Giants, participated in a formal workout with the Chicago White Sox at their training grounds in Pasadena. Jimmy Dykes, the manager of the Sox who had watched Robinson's play over the past several seasons, was happy to have them. "Personally, I would welcome Negro players on the Sox," he said, "and I believe every one of the other 15 big-league managers would do likewise. As for the players, they'd all get along too."[5] It was another chink in baseball's segregated armor, but for Robinson it seemed all too small.

Robinson immediately passed the Army's physical exam and was sent on to Fort Riley, Kansas for basic training. It was 13 weeks of grueling physical exertion designed to make a soldier out of any man healthy enough to begin the program. Robinson excelled there. He received high marks on the firing range and according to military records was well regarded for his character. Once basic training was complete, Private Robinson remained at Fort Riley, assigned to one of the few remaining cavalry units in the Army. His major duty: holding the horses' heads still as they were vaccinated. It wasn't exactly what he'd expected of military life.

As soon as he could, Robinson applied for Officer's Candidate School (OCS). For a college-educated athlete who had performed so well in basic training, this should have been a matter of course. But not, it seemed, for an African American man with these qualifications. Robinson's OCS application, along with those of others from his segregated unit, stalled. The U.S. military remained divided along color lines, and many of its officers were convinced that black men were simply not capable of military leadership. Blacks were not banned from the officers' ranks outright, but neither were they uniformly welcomed. Robinson, fuming, waited for three long months for the Army to take action on his application. His questions and complaints to his higher-ups got no response.[6]

Then world heavyweight boxing champion Joe Louis arrived at Fort Riley on temporary assignment. Louis was a global celebrity, a true American hero who in 1938 had stood up to Nazi Germany in the person of Max Schmeling, the German boxing champ, and won. After Pearl Harbor, he volunteered for military service.

When Louis learned that another celebrated athlete was on the base, he sought Robinson out. The two men began to work out together and became good friends. It wasn't long before Louis heard all about the OCS dilemma. He knew just the strings to pull, and the Fort Riley brass came under some uncomfortable scrutiny. Suddenly the delay ended, and Robinson and his buddies began OCS training. They were part of the first integrated OCS class in U.S. Army history, and by contemporary accounts, Robinson was an especially well-liked member of the group. On January 28, 1943, he completed his OCS training and accepted his commission as a second lieutenant in the cavalry. A few weeks later he presented a small diamond ring to Rachel, and they formally announced their engagement.

THE WAR WITHIN THE WAR

Assigned the job of morale officer in a truck battalion, Robinson had to mediate a continuing series of problems between the men of his segregated unit and the Fort Riley brass. Black soldiers, and by extension African Americans across the country, were becoming increasingly agitated about the pervasive discrimination within the military. Thousands of blacks had been drafted and trained for combat, but none of them were being permitted to fight on the front lines of the war. Instead, they were relegated to service duties, a huge blow to their pride. Black soldiers and officers were rarely accorded the respect that the uniform deserved, and violence against them seemed to be escalating. Especially on bases in the South, separate and unequal facilities were the rule.

The daily injustice that most irritated the black soldiers of Fort Riley was that the Post Exchange had only six or seven seats available for them. Dozens of tables were reserved for the white men of the base, and often the black soldiers had to stand even though seats in the white section were empty. Robinson decided to do something about it. He telephoned the provost marshal, a major, and explained the situation, but the major refused to consider making any changes. Robinson pressed him for a reason. "Finally, taking it for granted that I was white, [the major] said, 'Lieutenant, let me put it to you this way. How would you like to have your wife sitting next to a nigger?'"[7]

Robinson exploded, shouting at the major at the top of his voice until the man hung up. Then he took the matter to his superior officer, Colonel Longley. Longley was sympathetic, and he made the black soldiers' request a personal cause. More seats were given over to their section of the P/X, though the facility remained strictly segregated, and the provost marshal was rebuked for his reflexive racism.[8]

Robinson's outspokenness in this racial cause didn't seem to bother his higher-ups, but his stance on another matter did. Military posts and bases often organized football and baseball teams that would compete against other bases or local colleges. The teams' performances were a source of great pride to the bases' commanders, who took their bragging rights very seriously. Generally, these squads were closed to blacks—that spring Robinson had been turned away from the Fort Riley baseball team, which included his future Brooklyn teammate Pete Reiser—but to the colonel in charge of the football team, the idea of playing a former all-American, even a black one, was intoxicating. Robinson practiced with the squad in preparation for its fall season.

He was surprised, then, to be given an unexpected two-week furlough just when the team was about to play its first game. Then he figured it out: that first game was against the University of Missouri, which had refused to take the field if a black man was to share it. Rather than stand up for Robinson or tell him the truth, the colonel had sent him off the base.

Robinson used his two weeks to visit his family in Pasadena and to see Rachel in San Francisco, where she was attending nursing school. When he returned to Fort Riley, he reported to the colonel/coach and quit the team, saying that he would not play in any games if he was barred from some contests on account of his race.[9] His refusal won him few friends on the base.

Robinson stayed for several more uncomfortable months at Fort Riley, waiting for transfer into a unit that would be sent overseas. (The Army had finally decided to send some black soldiers to the front lines.) He spent a good deal of time agonizing over his relationship with Rachel. They had fought a heated long-distance argument over her desire to join the Army's Nurse Cadet Corps. He, jealous, felt that the corps would expose his beloved to the temptations of other men; she was grieving her missing brother Chuck, a military pilot who had disappeared somewhere in Europe, and wanted to take some part in the fight. In February, Rachel ended their engagement. Robinson promptly found himself a rebound girlfriend, but he was miserable over the breakup.

In April 1944, in the midst of this emotional turmoil, Robinson was transferred to Camp Hood, Texas and attached to a platoon in the all-black 761st Tank Battalion. He had no experience in mechanized warfare: all his training had been with horses. But horses weren't being sent to fight in Europe—tanks were. The men under his command were preparing to combat the Nazis' terrifying Panzer tank divisions. The training they received here in Texas was literally a matter of life and death. Robinson decided that they deserved his honesty.

"I called them out and lined them up," he related later. "'Men,' I said, 'I know nothing about tanks, nothing at all. I am asking you to help me out in this unusual situation.' There was a deep and impressive silence . . . 'The sergeant is in command of this group,' I said, pointing to the amazed man beside me."[10]

While the men were taken aback by his straightforwardness, Robinson felt that they appreciated it. They threw themselves into their training maneuvers, and the sergeant took care to teach Robinson as they went along. Before long the battalion commander, Lieutenant Colonel Paul L. Bates, noticed the unit's excellent teamwork and efficient operations, which stood out even within the notably fierce and proud 761st Battalion. An especially fair-minded white man, Bates made a point to compliment Robinson on the platoon's success. The junior officer confessed the whole story, and his forthrightness impressed Bates even more.

In July and August, the 761st was set to deploy to the European theater. Robinson was on limited duty because of a flare-up of his old ankle injury and did not have to serve in combat if he did not wish to. Bates, however, was so taken with Robinson's work that he asked him to consider coming along to Europe as his morale officer. Combat duty would bring lucrative benefits and additional pay, along of course with great risks. Robinson found the decision a difficult one. He underwent several rounds of x-rays, diagnoses, and treatments during a lengthy stay at a hospital just outside the base to determine if active-duty status was possible for him.

THE BACK OF THE BUS: ROBINSON'S COURT-MARTIAL

On the night of July 6, after a visit to the black officers' club at Camp Hood, Robinson boarded a camp bus, which the Army provided to help its men get around the massive installation. Robinson would take this vehicle to the gates of the camp, where he could transfer to a public bus back to the hospital. As he boarded, Robinson chatted with Virginia Jones, the wife of a fellow black officer. She lived near the hospital, and he had offered to escort her home. The two sat together in a seat in the center of the bus.

When the bus driver noticed this, he was incensed. Here was a black man sitting in the middle of a bus, not in the back rows, as was the law throughout the South. Moreover, he was sitting next to a light-skinned woman—Mrs. Jones, though she was African American herself, had a light complexion and was often taken for white. "Hey, you," the driver called out, "move to the rear of the bus!"[11]

Robinson was confused at first, then embarrassed, then angry. He knew that the Army had recently issued an order desegregating the buses on all its bases, even those in the South. What really hurt, though, was that his status as a second lieutenant in the U.S. Army clearly meant nothing to this bigoted man. "Apparently Jim Crow was Jim Crow to the bus driver, army uniform or no uniform."[12] Robinson informed him of the Army's desegregation rule and refused to move.

When the bus came to the end of the line, the driver leaped out, swearing to "fix" the mouthy black man who would not ride in the back of the bus. He called the military police (MPs) as the bus emptied, and passengers joined in the argument. Robinson became more and more agitated as the MPs brought him to their headquarters to see the provost marshal. When he heard a private refer to him as a "nigger lieutenant," he exploded, shouting that "if he ever called me a nigger again I would break him in two."[13]

Further indignities awaited at the office of the assistant provost marshal, Captain Gerald M. Bear. Bear seemed uninterested in Robinson's version of events. He listened first to the stories told by the white MPs, who had seen only the argument outside the bus and had not been present for the exchange with the bus driver that had started it all. When Robinson finally gave his statement, Bear allowed his civilian stenographer to scold Robinson for having the temerity to choose his own bus seat. When Robinson objected to the stenographer's comments, Bear called him an "uppity nigger" and rebuked him for speaking to a woman in such an angry tone.[14] There was no doubt in Robinson's mind that he was being rail-roaded into a court-martial, a military trial.

Charged with a laundry list of offenses—insubordination, disturbing the peace, drunkenness, conduct unbecoming an officer, insulting a civilian, refusing to obey a superior officer—the court-martial orders were referred to Robinson's commander, Lt. Col. Bates. Bates refused to sign them. Robinson was promptly transferred to the 758th Battalion, whose commander pushed the court-martial papers through. If convicted, Robinson would be dishonorably discharged, a blot on his record that, he feared, would make future employment next to impossible.

Word of his predicament spread quickly through the ranks of the black officers and soldiers at Camp Hood and beyond. Outraged, many of them wrote to the National Association for the Advancement of Colored People (NAACP) and to black newspapers like the *Chicago Defender* and the *Pittsburgh Courier*. Reporters called Camp Hood seeking comment. One of California's senators wrote to the Secretary of War about the situation. It became increasingly clear to the Camp Hood brass that the Robinson matter was "full of dynamite," as one commander there put it.[15]

The court-martial was set for August 2. The first Army attorney assigned to Robinson, a young white Southern man, was honest enough to admit that he could not be impartial in a trial that tested the rules of segregation. "To my great and thankful admiration," Robinson said later, "he brought in another officer to act as my lawyer." A team of three officer-attorneys handled the defense at the hearing.[16]

By the time of the trial, the charges against Robinson had been modified, in part a result of all the outside pressure. Now he faced accusations of insubordination and willful disobedience, charges that carried a fine and not a discharge if he was convicted. They could, however, be difficult to disprove: these charges stemmed from the scene in Captain Bear's office, not from the bus incident, and there were no outside witnesses to them. It was Robinson's word against that of Bear and his staff.

The court-martial, heard by a panel of nine senior officers, lasted four hours. Robinson, Bear, and members of his staff testified and were cross-examined. The defense team's case rested on the theory that Robinson had not been insubordinate to Bear, but that Bear had given confusing and contradictory orders in the heat of the moment. Robinson's attorneys managed to catch inconsistencies in Bear's and others' statements that confirmed Robinson's account of the night. And they gave him a chance to humanize his plight while on the stand by exploring why he objected to being called "nigger," a point that seemed to perplex all of the whites he had encountered.

"My grandmother gave me a good definition" of the word, Robinson said. "She was a slave, and she said the definition of the word was a low, uncouth person, and pertains to no one in particular; but I don't consider that I am low and uncouth...I do not consider myself a nigger at all, I am a negro, but not a nigger."[17]

The defense team also called Colonel Bates as a character witness. Bates' praise for the lieutenant was unstinting, and he stated emphatically that he would be proud to fight with Robinson in combat. Later, Robinson credited Bates' testimony as the factor that tipped the balance. The judges quickly found him "not guilty of all specifications and charges."[18]

Now that he was free, Robinson found himself at loose ends within the Army. The 761st Battalion was already on its way to Europe, where its men became the first black armored unit to fight for the United States. Under General George S. Patton, they would storm through France, Belgium, Germany, and Austria and would help liberate the concentration camp at Buchenwald. Robinson would not be with the men he had once led. Disillusioned, he requested to be placed on reserve or inactive status. On November 28, after a transfer to Camp Breckenridge in Kentucky and short-term attachments to several different units, he was "honorably relieved of active duty by reason of physical disqualification."[19]

No doubt Robinson was glad to say goodbye to Army life. Returning home to Pasadena, he was battered but unbowed. "I had learned that I was in two wars," he would say later, "one against the foreign enemy, and the other against prejudice at home."[20]

NOTES

1. Jackie Robinson, *I Never Had It Made* (New York: Ecco, 1995), p. 11.

2. Jackie Robinson as told to Ed Reid, "Robinson Finds Louis Real Champ," *Washington Post*, August 25, 1949, p. 17.

3. *Pasadena Star-News*, October 26, 1977. Cited in Arnold Rampersad, *Jackie Robinson: A Biography* (New York: Ballantine Books, 1998), p. 85.

4. Jules Tygiel, *Baseball's Great Experiment* (New York: Oxford University Press, 1997), p. 61.

5. *Daily Worker*, March 23, 1942. Cited in David Falkner, *Great Time Coming* (New York: Simon and Schuster, 1995), p. 68.

6. Robinson, *I Never Had It Made*, p. 13.

7. Robinson, *I Never Had It Made*, p. 14.

8. Robinson, *I Never Had It Made*, p. 16.

9. Robinson, *I Never Had It Made*, p. 17.

10. Robinson, "Robinson Finds Louis Real Champ," *Washington Post*, August 25, 1949, p. 17.

11. Jackie Robinson as told to Ed Reid, "Robinson Arrested, Court-Martialed," *Washington Post*, August 26, 1949, p. B5.

12. Robinson, "Robinson Arrested, Court-Martialed," *Washington Post*, August 26, 1949, p. B5.

13. Jules Tygiel, "The Court-Martial of Jackie Robinson," *American Heritage*, September 1984, pp. 34–39.

14. Robinson, *I Never Had It Made*, p. 20.

15. Arnold Rampersad, *Jackie Robinson: A Biography* (New York: Ballantine Books, 1998), p. 104.

16. Jackie Robinson as told to Ed Reid, "Robinson Cleared of Charges in Army," *Washington Post*, August 27, 1949, p. 10; Rampersad, *Jackie Robinson*.

17. Rampersad, *Jackie Robinson*, p. 108.

18. Tygiel, "The Court-Martial of Jackie Robinson."

19. Rampersad, *Jackie Robinson*, p. 111.

20. Jackie Robinson, *Baseball Has Done It* (Brooklyn, NY: Ig Publishing, 2005), p. 49.

Chapter 4

BASEBALL CALLING,
1945–1946

Back at Pepper Street, Robinson moped. He had no job and no real idea of what he would do next. And while he hardly wanted to admit it, he missed Rachel and regretted the end of their relationship. Mallie could see how unhappy he was and pleaded with him to get in touch with the girl she had liked so much. Finally, he called Rachel in San Francisco. She had been just as unable to get over their breakup and was glad to hear from him. She had good news to share, too: her brother was alive after all and was on his way home from Europe. Robinson raced north to meet her for a joyous reunion, and they renewed their engagement.

Meanwhile, some career possibilities were developing. Robinson's old friend and mentor, Rev. Karl Downs, had returned to Texas to become the president of Samuel Huston College, a small black school in Austin. Downs offered Robinson a job as the college's athletic director.

At the same time, Robinson was exchanging letters with the owner of the Kansas City Monarchs, the premier team of the Negro National League. He had met a Monarchs pitcher, Ted Alexander, at Camp Breckenridge in his final days in the service and had heard that the owner, Thomas Y. Baird, was looking to hire. Robinson was wary of the Negro Leagues; not only had he been cheated out of a day's pay by barnstormers years before, he was uneasy about the contract-free handshake deals that were standard procedure. Still, the money was good. After some haggling, Baird offered Robinson $100 a week to play baseball in the spring, and Robinson accepted. By mid-December Robinson was in Austin, trying to set up a basketball team for Downs' school. In April he would head to Houston and join the Monarchs for the season.

With the war still on, Samuel Huston College was woefully short of young men. Only 30 or 40 male students were enrolled there, out of a student body of about 300. When Robinson put out the call for basketball tryouts, just seven potential players showed up. Still, Robinson persevered, no doubt feeling that Rev. Downs deserved his best effort. He set up the college's first physical education program and molded his little group of basketball players into a team. When they defeated their conference's defending champion in a 61–59 upset, it was as sweet a victory as any he had achieved on the court.

THE NEGRO LEAGUES

Once the college basketball season ended, Robinson moved on to Houston as planned to meet up with the Monarchs. One of the original and most storied teams of the Negro Leagues, the Monarchs' roster had included such legends as Satchel Paige, "Cool Papa" Bell, Hilton Smith, Willard "Home Run" Brown, Newt Allen, and Buck O'Neil. The club drew great crowds wherever it went, it was a perennial postseason contender, and it paid its players better than most of the other teams in the league. As a team, the Monarchs possessed a storehouse of baseball strategy and lore that they shared freely with one another during the long overnight bus rides that took them from game to game. Robinson would soon begin a season-long crash course in the art of baseball as he listened in on the players' "skull sessions," during which they picked apart each contest and prepared for the next day's game.

Almost as soon as he joined the team, he was singled out for a special mission. Wendell Smith, a reporter for the *Pittsburgh Courier*, had chosen Boston as the new target of his long-running baseball-integration campaign. With the help of a crusading city councilman, Isadore Muchnick, Smith got the Boston Red Sox to agree to a tryout for black ballplayers. (The Sox had claimed that they would be thrilled to sign a black player, but sadly none cared to join the team. Smith was going to call their bluff with a few prospects.) Smith rounded up Robinson, Marvin Williams of the Philadelphia Stars, and Sam Jethroe of the Cleveland Buckeyes and brought them all to Boston. The three black athletes put on an impressive show in Fenway Park, crowned by Robinson's assault on the Green Monster, the ballpark's looming left-field wall. Muchnick said later, "You never saw anyone hit The Wall the way Robinson did that day. Bang, bang, bang: he rattled it."[1] The fireworks were completely ignored by Boston's management, which was not seriously interested in integration and would in fact resist hiring black players longer than any other major-league club. But the farcical tryout did give Smith and Robinson a chance to get to know one another. The influential Smith became convinced that if anyone was to make a successful attack on the color line, Robinson would be the man.

Robinson headed back to Kansas City and the rigors of a season in the Negro Leagues. The schedule was demanding: mixed in with the 62 official league games would be scores of unofficial games pitting the Monarchs against semi-pro squads or barnstorming major leaguers. It meant that the team was almost constantly on the road, and for a group of black men, that was rarely a comfortable place to be. The team had to travel in its own overcrowded bus, which due to Jim Crow segregation laws often served as a communal hotel room as well. Restaurants would not serve them. Gas stations would not allow them to use their restrooms. After his fraught experience in the Army, the endless injustice of it all made Robinson furious. In later years, he would complain about low player salaries, unprofessional umpiring, and the owners' shady business dealings and would declare that "Negro baseball . . . needs a housecleaning from top to bottom."[2]

Nonetheless, Robinson performed well as a Monarch, hitting an estimated .345 (statistics were never reliably kept in Negro League contests) and running the bases with all his old agility. He wasn't regarded as an outstanding fielder, but he became the team's regular shortstop, and he was chosen to start in the East-West All-Star game in July. But he never felt entirely comfortable with the other members of his team. He was one of the few Negro Leaguers with any college education and the only one who had attended a predominantly white university. Still a devout Methodist, he did not smoke or drink, and he disapproved of the late-night partying that was the norm among the other players. Some of his teammates would remember Robinson as humble, modest, and eager to learn the finer points of a game that had not been his top priority in high school or college. Others, perhaps sensing his unhappiness, found him aloof and distant. Still others would recall his rage at the segregation he encountered at every turn.

As the summer wound down, Robinson was not sure if he would continue to pursue his professional baseball career beyond this single season. Rachel, who had graduated from nursing school that spring and had taken a job at a Los Angeles hospital, did not intend to marry a man who would be on the road so much of the time. He did not expect that the integration campaign of Wendell Smith and the other journalists would bear fruit anytime soon. And he did not know that he was being closely watched by scouts from the Brooklyn Dodgers.

BRANCH RICKEY'S "GREAT EXPERIMENT"

World War II had changed the way many Americans thought about race. Black and white workers had toiled side by side in shipyards and factories on the home front; black soldiers had performed heroically in combat. The exclusion of black athletes from baseball came increasingly into question. Sports columnists for major daily newspapers, including Jimmy Cannon in the *New York Post* and Dick Young in the *New York Daily News*, began to write about the topic that Wendell Smith and others had been discussing for so long. Several cities, including New York and Boston, were debating fair employment laws that would outlaw racial bias in hiring—and that would extend to the baseball teams based in those towns.

In this atmosphere, Branch Rickey, the president and general manager of the Brooklyn Dodgers, put in motion what he called the "Great Experiment": his plan to integrate baseball. By all accounts one of the sharpest baseball minds ever, Rickey had spent much of his career with the St. Louis Cardinals. There he invented the farm system, the network of minor-league ballclubs that teams still use today to nurture, and contractually control, young athletic talent. When Rickey came to the Dodgers in 1942, he took charge of a team that was weak on prospects, and his first task was to pack the system with young, eager kids. A practical man, he knew that the African American talent pool would be a rich source for Brooklyn to tap. Rickey was idealistic and religious as well. Abraham Lincoln was his idol, and he aspired to be an emancipator within the baseball world. Later, he would explain his purpose simply: "First, to win a pennant. I think there's some good colored players. The second reason is...it's right!"[3]

Rickey moved slowly at first, starting in 1942 and 1943, to build support for integration within the Dodgers organization and to develop sympathetic contacts in the press, including Wendell Smith. In the spring of 1945, feeling that the time was ripe, he quietly gathered up the names of likely candidates. Fresh from the Boston tryout, Smith recommended Robinson as not only a terrific athlete, but a man of character. "[Robinson] was tough, he was intelligent, and he was proud," concurred Clyde Sukeforth, one of the Dodgers' top scouts.[4] Robinson had played on integrated teams in the past; he was college educated; he had been an officer in the Army; he had no potentially embarrassing personal habits. He went straight to the top of Rickey's list.

That summer, three different Dodgers scouts went out to watch Robinson and several other Negro Leaguers play. As a cover story, Rickey announced that he planned to form a new Negro ballclub, the Brooklyn

Brown Dodgers, as part of a third Negro League. The scouts sent back good reports on Robinson, but they pointed out one serious personality flaw: his tendency to anger. Rickey checked it out with Smith. "I didn't want to tell Mr. Rickey, 'Yes, he's tough to get along with,'" Smith recalled. "A lot of us knew that. When he was aroused, Jackie had a sizable temper. But to survive, he couldn't be a Mickey Mouse."[5] Rickey seems to have agreed, because in late August he sent Sukeforth out to observe Robinson one more time and then bring him back to Brooklyn for an interview. If Robinson could not come to New York, Rickey said that he would travel to wherever the Monarchs were. (At that, Sukeforth would say later, "I'm not the smartest guy in the world, but I said to myself, *this could be the real thing.*"[6])

Sukeforth found the team in Chicago's Comiskey Park. Robinson was sidelined with a sore shoulder; he would be out for a week. It seemed like an opportune moment. A day or two later, the two men met up in Toledo, Ohio and boarded a train for New York.

Robinson had been suspicious when Sukeforth first approached him. The Boston experience had soured him on overtures from "organized" baseball. But the Dodger scout convinced him that he was on the lookout for Brown Dodgers talent, and Robinson—now 26 years old, hardly young as baseball prospects go—wondered if he would be asked to be the new team's manager. Then Sukeforth told him that Rickey had been willing to travel to see him, and Robinson had an inkling of another possibility, one he had never expected to see in his lifetime. "The significance of that last part wasn't lost on him, I could see that," Sukeforth remembered.[7]

On August 28, Sukeforth escorted Robinson to Montague Street in Brooklyn and into the office of Branch Rickey. The room was dominated by a huge blackboard that bore the name of every player currently toiling within the Dodgers system, from the rookie leagues to the big leagues. A portrait of Lincoln looked down from another wall. What felt like long minutes stretched out as Rickey and Robinson held one another's gaze. Suddenly, Rickey broke the silence: "Do you have a girl?"

"That stunned me," Robinson remembered. "I wondered if Mr. Rickey had brought me all the way from Chicago to talk about my love life. 'I don't know,' I said. I tried to explain that I hadn't been able to see Rachel since I joined the Monarchs, and I didn't know whether I had a girl or not.

"'Of course you have a girl,' Mr. Rickey said, 'and you ought to marry her as quick as you can.'"[8] Then he revealed what Robinson may have suspected but still could not quite believe: that he was being offered the opportunity to become the first black man in the modern history of major-league baseball. Specifically, he had the chance to play for the Montreal Royals, Brooklyn's top farm team, and if he could succeed there, the Dodgers would be his next stop.

The path would not be a smooth one, Rickey warned. The other owners, the umpires, other ball clubs and fans, even many teammates and Brooklyn rooters would hope for and expect his failure. "We can win," Rickey told him, "only if I can convince the world that I'm doing this because you're a great ballplayer and a fine gentleman."[9]

For the next three hours the Dodgers president graphically described all the dangers and humiliations Robinson would be forced to confront. Rickey took on the persona of an insulting hotel clerk refusing a room, an angry fan spewing racial hate, a malicious teammate, a vicious opponent sliding into him with his spikes. It took great force of will for the fiercely proud Robinson not to react. "His acting was so convincing I found myself chain-gripping my fingers behind my back," he remembered.[10]

Robinson was being asked to set aside his right to retaliate—a right he had always believed to be at the very root of his personal dignity. The man who was court-martialed rather than move to the back of a bus, who had gone to jail rather than slink away from a bullying police officer, could hardly believe his ears.

"'Mr. Rickey,' I asked, 'are you looking for a Negro who is afraid to fight back?' I never will forget the way he exploded.

"'Robinson,' he said, 'I'm looking for a ballplayer with guts enough not to fight back.'"[11]

As the conversation continued, both men drew on their shared Christian faith as a guide. They talked about turning the other cheek and about the strength of nonresistance. Robinson took his time before coming to a conclusion. At last he said, "Mr. Rickey, I think I can play ball in Montreal. I think I can play ball in Brooklyn. But, you're a better judge of that than I am. If you want to take this gamble, I will promise you there will be no incident."[12]

That very afternoon Robinson signed an agreement that would lead to a signing bonus of $3,500 and a $600-per-month salary with Montreal. He was sworn to secrecy (though Rickey allowed him to tell Rachel and his mother) and, dazed, headed back to the train station to rejoin the Monarchs.

He found the playing and living conditions of the Negro Leagues even harder to take now than before his trip to Brooklyn, however. Within a few days he jumped the team and went home to California. There, he tried to describe for Mallie and for Rachel the changes that were on the horizon for him and for them all. They could barely comprehend it. Racial integration of the kind he was describing seemed beyond imagining. For Rachel, the change that this would mean in the life she had expected—from West Coast to East, from nurse to full-time baseball wife, from dignified anonymity to unpredictable notoriety—was tremendous.

They set a February wedding date, but to give herself a little time and space, Rachel arranged to make a several-week visit to New York City in the fall with a friend from nursing school. Robinson had signed on for a barnstorming trip to Venezuela with other Negro Leaguers that would take place at the same time.

Rickey, meanwhile, had hoped to quietly sign several more Negro League players, then announce them all when spring training approached. He had not figured on New York City politics getting in his way. In the political campaigns that fall, several candidates, including Mayor Fiorello LaGuardia, talked about using state anti-discrimination laws to force baseball integration. The last thing Rickey, a staunch conservative, wanted was to look as if the state had forced him to do anything. He arranged a press conference in Montreal on October 23. Robinson, who was in New York to spend time with Rachel and meet his barnstorming team, flew north, "nervous as the devil," to be there.[13]

About two dozen reporters were present when Hector Racine, the president of the Montreal Royals, began to speak that morning. He introduced Branch Rickey Jr., the director of the Dodger farm system. And he introduced Jack Roosevelt Robinson, who had just signed his formal contract with Montreal. The shocked reporters sat silent for a moment. Then the room burst into noise and activity as they rose and ran for the telephones to get the news out as quickly as possible.

Racine and Rickey gave statements when the writers had settled down again, emphasizing Robinson's skill as an athlete and noting that those who were already prejudiced, both within and outside baseball, would be bound to criticize his signing. Robinson himself charmed the reporters with a few modest words: "Of course, I can't begin to tell you how happy I am that I am the first member of my race in organized ball. I realize how much it means to me, to my race, and to baseball. I can only say I'll do my very best to come through in every manner."[14]

In public and in print, most baseball men reacted to Robinson's signing diplomatically. If integration was going to happen, they would rather see it happen on someone else's team first. Anyway, Robinson still had to play his way out of the minor leagues. Some Negro League owners, especially Baird of the Monarchs, were furious. They feared losing their best players and eventually their businesses to white baseball. Baird threatened to sue, claiming breach of contract. But the reaction of most of the black press and fans to Robinson's signing was so ecstatic that Baird soon realized his team could suffer a huge backlash if he stood in the way of the man who was "the symbol of hope for millions of colored people in this country and elsewhere," as the NAACP's magazine *The Crisis* put it.[15]

Not a few of the Negro Leaguers privately questioned the choice of Robinson, though they were publicly supportive. The great Satchel Paige said that Robinson's signing "hurt me deep down...I'd been the one who everybody'd said should be in the majors."[16] Hilton Smith believed it wasn't Robinson's baseball skills that had gotten him signed; it was that "he had played football with white boys."[17] Some of the more conspiracy-minded players feared that the Dodgers had deliberately signed a less-talented black man so that, when he failed, they could go back to their segregated ways.

In early November, Robinson's barnstorming team launched their 24-game South American schedule. The group was made up of experienced veterans, including first baseman Buck Leonard, catcher Quincy Trouppe, outfielder Sam Jethroe, third baseman Parnell Woods, and catcher Roy Campanella. But the best-known among them was the rookie Jackie Robinson. Some on the tour reached out to Robinson to offer tips or advice—after all, if he succeeded in opening the door to the major leagues, they might be next. He didn't always take to their well-meant schooling. As always, he was uncomfortable in the larger group, but one-on-one he would drop his defensiveness.

Gene Benson of the Philadephia Stars was Robinson's roommate on the tour, and to him the younger man was "just a swell person." Benson worked with Robinson on hitting the curveball, which had been a huge liability during his season with the Monarchs. Robinson learned fast: while keeping his own straight-up batting stance, he worked on keeping his hands back, as Benson advised, and became an excellent curveball hitter. Benson was also able to reassure Robinson that he could certainly compete in "the other league." "I told him one day, if you can hit .200 in this league, you might be able to hit .300 in the other one." The reason? "Everything that's outlawed in their league is allowed in ours. In our league, for example, throwing at you is just part of the game...they're not gonna brush you back, they're gonna throw at you. I told him about the spitball: it's outlawed in their league, not in ours."[18] As far as Benson was concerned, all this made the Negro Leagues much harder for a hitter. And Robinson had hit .345 in the Negro Leagues.

Meanwhile, Rickey was following through on his original plan to sign additional black ballplayers to minor-league contracts. Pitcher John Wright of the Homestead Grays, fastballer Don Newcombe of the Newark Eagles, and Campanella all joined the Dodgers system that winter and spring.

THE FIRST INTEGRATED SPRING TRAINING

Robinson returned to the States in January, met Rachel in New York, and traveled back to Los Angeles with her by train for their February 10 wedding. Zellee Isum had been hard at work planning the day. She had reserved the Independent Church of Christ, the largest black church in the city, and put together "a pageant, an extravaganza," Rachel would say later. It wasn't quite what the bride had wanted, but the spectacle gave her mother such joy that Rachel could hardly refuse it.[19] Karl Downs flew in from Austin to officiate; Jack Gordon was best man. The church was packed with family and with friends from UCLA, members of the Pepper Street Gang, and former coaches and teammates. Rachel's brother Chuck walked her down the aisle.

The happy pair spent their two-week honeymoon in San Jose, staying in Rachel's aunt's house and visiting friends and family in the area. Looming over them both was the greatest challenge either of them had yet faced: the first integrated spring training in modern history, set to be held in the towns of Daytona Beach and Sanford, Florida. Sanford, about 20 miles from Daytona Beach, was the site of the minor league teams' pre-training camps. After a week or so there, they would move to Daytona Beach, where they and the Dodgers would play exhibition games and do additional conditioning.

Rickey had tried to make things as comfortable as possible for Robinson and for Wright, who were both set to train with the Montreal team. Daytona Beach, the home of black educator-activist Mary McLeod Bethune, had a reputation as a racially tolerant city (in comparison, at least, with the brutally segregated communities that surrounded it). Rickey had insisted that Rachel come along to spring training, even though most wives remained at home. He'd hired Wendell Smith to be Robinson's companion and protector, and Smith made good use of his contacts to secure a room for the Robinsons in the home of a prominent local black family.

Rickey could not control everything, however. The Robinsons' travel arrangements were beyond him, and their trip to Florida was a frustrating ordeal for them both. They left Los Angeles by plane on February 28, planning to transfer at New Orleans and arrive in Daytona Beach on March 1, the day Robinson was set to report to camp. But when they disembarked in New Orleans, they were bumped from one connecting flight and then another, and were given poor excuses each time. "Another typical black experience," Robinson noted. It took twelve hours for the airline to find a flight with seats for them. When that plane touched down in Pensacola, Florida, they were removed from the flight again, this time quite clearly so that a white couple could fly instead.[20]

They gave up on the airlines and decided to catch a bus to Daytona Beach. It was a 16-hour ride, most of it spent in the hard, uncomfortable, nonreclining bench seats in the back. "I buried my head behind the seat in front of me and began to cry," Rachel remembered. She had never experienced this kind of humiliation. But in the early morning hours, as the back of the bus filled with working people, she saw kindness as they helped one another and took turns sharing the few available seats. "Now I understood about how black folks living under those terrible conditions really had to look out for one another, or we would all of us go down. I began to feel a great bond I had never felt before...I think I was much more ready now to deal with the world we had entered."[21]

When they finally got off the bus in Daytona, a full day late, Robinson was on the verge of quitting. Smith, who met them at the bus station with a photographer, talked him down. They and John Wright were warmly welcomed into the homes of black families in Sanford. By the morning of Monday, March 4, Robinson was ready to play ball.

That first day of spring training wasn't anything out of the ordinary. Robinson and Wright joined about 200 hopeful ballplayers in the bumpy, open field that served as the Sanford practice facility. They stretched and ran, did calisthenics, took a little batting practice, and joined in a few pepper games. It was so anticlimactic, few newspapers covered it. One of those that did was the *Daily Worker*, which had championed integrated baseball for so long. "It was a thrilling day," said its sports editor, Bill Mardo. "The day belonged to decent-minded people who understood that discrimination against a man because of his skin hurt the nation as a whole."[22]

Clyde Sukeforth greeted Robinson, who was glad to see his familiar face, and introduced him and Wright to Montreal manager Clay Hopper. Many sources assert that the Mississippi-born and bred Hopper had pleaded with Rickey not to make him accept black players on his team and even asked Rickey, "Do you really think a nigger's a human being?"[23] In fact, Hopper was hired to manage the Royals after Robinson had signed his contract to play for the team, so whatever his objections to managing an integrated squad, they did not prevent him from taking the job. He and Rickey had a long history together, and it seems certain that part of Rickey's "Great Experiment" called for Southerners like Hopper to take key roles in the drama.

First, though, Robinson had work to do. He had to get into playing shape, perform well enough to make the Montreal roster, and push past the six shortstops already in camp, including Stan Bréard, who had been the regular shortstop in 1945 and was popular among his fellow French Canadians. Even more difficult, after two uneventful days of pre-training camp, rumors spread that a mob of angry whites was about to march on the home where he and Rachel were staying. The whole operation had to pull up stakes and retreat to Daytona Beach. Since the Royals had been scheduled to move to Daytona Beach the next week anyway, the threat was not reported in the press. But it certainly put added stress on Robinson and on Wright. Robinson's hitting was especially weak, and each day he failed to do well at the plate added to his and to Rachel's worry that he might be cut from the roster.

In Daytona Beach on March 17, Robinson was in the Montreal lineup when the squad played the Dodgers. It was, as one report had it, "the first time a Negro has ever played against a big league team in the South."[24] The little ballpark was packed with a capacity crowd of 4,000, at least a quarter of whom were African American. Robinson was starting at second base in this game in his effort to make the ballclub at any position. He was hitless in the game, but his defense was superb. "He looked like a real ballplayer out there," said Dodgers manager Leo Durocher after the game. "Don't forget he was under terrific pressure...But he came through it like a champion."[25]

Several of Robinson's fellow players, as well as Rickey himself, were helping him learn how to field his new position at second. Robinson's intelligence and athleticism made him an excellent student. "In one half hour he learned to make the double play pivot correctly," another infielder noted with approval and a touch of amazement.[26]

After the game against the Dodgers, Robinson felt better about his progress and began to hit the ball with more confidence. When authorities in Jacksonville, Florida sent the Dodgers word that local regulations prohibited mixed-race ballgames, Rickey and the Royals backed Robinson and Wright up: the team would cancel exhibition games rather than play without them. Several of the squad's "away" games that spring would be held in Daytona Beach instead after they were called off due to racism. Later, Robinson would write, "I was deeply embarrassed and upset by the trouble I was causing the Montreal club; I wanted to quit baseball before the season opened. But Rachel and Mr. Rickey talked me out of it."[27]

If anything, the hardship seemed to solidify the team and its management. When spring training ended, both Robinson and Wright were named to the roster of the Montreal Royals, and Hopper described his new second baseman as a "regular fella and a regular member of my baseball club."[28] On April 15 they boarded a train and headed north with the rest of the team to officially integrate the International League.

A ROYAL WELCOME

They opened the season on the road on April 18 against the Jersey City Giants. Just across the Hudson River from Manhattan, Jersey City, New Jersey was a tough industrial town that regarded its baseball team's Opening Day as a kind of local holiday. Its mayor gave city workers and school children the day off, and the whole town celebrated with marching bands and a pre-game parade. That year, though, Roosevelt Stadium was packed with out-of-towners as well. From Newark and Harlem, Brooklyn and Philadelphia, contingents of black fans descended on Jersey City to greet Jackie Robinson.

Robinson was nervous beyond words as the game began, and his first time up the best he could manage was a weak ground-out to short. When he came up again in the third inning with two men on, he attacked a first-pitch fastball and sent it soaring 340 feet over the left-field fence for a three-run home run. The crowd went mad; in the dugout, Wright laughed out loud. After Robinson crossed the plate, his teammates seemed to forget all about race as they congratulated him.[29]

He wasn't done. In the fifth inning, Robinson bunted for a single, then stole second and went to third on a teammate's grounder. Jersey City brought in a new pitcher, and Robinson went to work on him, dancing and feinting off the bag. Unnerved, the pitcher balked, which scored Robinson. When it was all over, Robinson had gone 4-for-5, with four runs scored and two stolen bases, in a 14–1 Montreal romp.

It was a fairytale beginning for a season that would be a tremendous success for Robinson, for Montreal, and for Rickey's experiment. More immediately, though, it was the first game of a two-week road trip that took the Royals to cities where many were deeply hostile to the idea of racial integration. In Syracuse, the opposing team released a black cat onto the playing field when Robinson was on deck as a crude sexual taunt. In Baltimore, race riots were predicted, though they never materialized, and Rachel had to sit silently in agony as men in the stands behind her called her husband a "nigger son of a bitch." "There wasn't anything I could say, but I took it all personally," she would recall.[30] On the road, the Royals attracted large African American crowds who reacted to Robinson's every move. He took their high expectations seriously; he felt that everything he did would reflect, for good or ill, on his whole race. All the pressure translated into sleepless nights and days of stress-induced nausea for Robinson. It would take a heavy toll on him later in his life, but this season he would only take a day or two off to rest.[31]

Things improved greatly when they arrived in Montreal. The Robinsons soon learned that there was little racial prejudice in Canada, simply because so few black people lived there. When Rachel went looking for an apartment, she braced herself for refusals and slammed doors. Instead, she found graciousness and friendly curiosity. She rented a furnished apartment in a French-speaking part of town, the East End. Despite the language barrier, the Robinsons' new neighbors went out of their way to assist them as they adjusted to the city. Rachel especially appreciated their help as the spring and summer went on—she was pregnant, to her husband's delight, and the neighbors' gifts of food and advice meant a great deal to her.

The Montreal fans were equally welcoming. They accepted the team's new second baseman with warmth and excitement.[32] Robinson arrived at Delormier Downs, the Royals' home field, two weeks into the season sporting a .371 batting average with eight stolen bases and 17 runs scored, and he would keep up that pace to help propel his team to the top of the International League. His fielding improved, too, as he got comfortable at second base. In May, he initiated 32 double plays in the Royals' 20 home games. On the basepaths, he put on such a show that the fans took to chanting "Allez! Steal that base!" whenever he got to first.[33]

The Royals gelled as a team as they continued to win, and during games many of his teammates vociferously defended Robinson from the insults he continued to hear from opponents. (True to his word to Rickey, Robinson refrained from doing any bench jockeying himself.) Socially, however, the white Royals went their own way. On the road, segregation kept them apart after games, but even in the team cafeteria at home, Robinson and Wright generally ate alone. When Wright was demoted to a single-A team on May 14, Robinson was really on his own. Only a few of his teammates reached out to him off the field. True integration was going to be a long time coming.

At the end of the season, the Royals, with a 19.5 game lead, won the International League crown easily. The team was strong in many respects, with excellent power and speed all through the lineup, but Robinson stood out. His will to win, the drive he had possessed since childhood, was obvious to fans and reporters and infectious on the field. Robinson won the league's batting title with a .349 average, led the league with 113 runs scored, and was second in stolen bases. When the season was over, he was named the International League's Most Valuable Player.

Before that, however, the Royals played the "Little World Series" against the Louisville Colonels, the American Association champions. Louisville, a typical Southern city, was strictly segregated. Robinson made history just by stepping onto the grass at Parkway Field for the first three games of the series. Black spectators filled their 466-seat portion of the stands to the bursting point, but they were drowned out by the jeers and abuse hurled by the white fans. "They called him watermelon eater, chicken thief, crap shooter, nigger, everything," a Colonels player recalled.[34] Robinson, sick at heart, got only one hit as Louisville won two out of three.

But when the series moved to Montreal, which was draped in several inches of snow, the fans leaped to his defense, soundly booing every Colonel who came to the plate. "I didn't approve of this kind of retaliation," Robinson would say later, "but I felt a jubilant sense of gratitude" at the Montrealers' spontaneous reaction.[35] The Royals rallied to take three straight, with Robinson supplying two game-winning hits, and won the series 4–2.

The celebration that followed was delirious. Fans swarmed the field and hoisted Robinson and Hopper to their shoulders. They finally allowed him to enter the locker room and dress, but they waited outside for him to reemerge, singing and cheering all the while. When he came out, reporters watched in amazement as a mass of fans reached out to Robinson, offering hugs, kisses, and pats on the back. He shouldered his way through the crowd as gently as he could, but finally he broke into a run. Five hundred cheering Montrealers followed him for three blocks until he hopped into a car that sped him out of their loving reach.[36]

NOTES

1. *Boston Herald*, April 16, 1987. Cited in Arnold Rampersad, *Jackie Robinson: A Biography* (New York: Ballantine Books, 1998), p. 120.

2. Jackie Robinson, "What's Wrong with Negro Baseball," *Ebony*, June 1948, pp. 16–24.

3. Jackie Robinson, *Baseball Has Done It* (Brooklyn, NY: Ig Publishing, 2005), p. 52.

4. Jules Tygiel, *Baseball's Great Experiment* (New York: Oxford University Press, 1997), p. 65.

5. Jerome Holtzman, "Jackie Robinson and the Great American Pastime," *Chicago Tribune*, April 11, 1993, p. C4.

6. Tygiel, *Baseball's Great Experiment*, p. 65.

7. Tygiel, *Baseball's Great Experiment*, p. 65.

8. Jackie Robinson, "Your Temper Can Ruin Us!" *Look*, February 22, 1955, pp. 78–87.

9. Carl T. Rowan with Jackie Robinson, *Wait Till Next Year* (New York: Random House, 1960), p. 4.

10. Tygiel, *Baseball's Great Experiment*, p. 66.

11. Robinson, *I Never Had It Made*, p. 33.

12. Tygiel, *Baseball's Great Experiment*, p. 67.

13. Tygiel, *Baseball's Great Experiment*, p. 72.

14. "Montreal Signs Negro Shortstop," *New York Times*, October 24, 1945, p. 17.

15. Bill L. Weaver, "The Black Press and the Assault on Professional Baseball's 'Color Line,' October, 1945-April, 1947," *Phylon*, Winter 1979, pp.303–317.

16. LeRoy (Satchel) Paige, *Maybe I'll Pitch Forever* (Garden City, N.Y.: Doubleday, 1962), p. 173.

17. Donn Rogosin, *Invisible Men: Life in Baseball's Negro Leagues* (New York: Atheneum, 1983), p. 214.

18. Falkner, *Great Time Coming*, pp. 121–123.

19. Rampersad, *Jackie Robinson*, p. 133.

20. Robinson, *I Never Had It Made*, pp. 39–40.

21. Rampersad, *Jackie Robinson*, pp. 138–139.

22. Chris Lamb, *Blackout: The Untold Story of Jackie Robinson's First Spring Training* (Lincoln: University of Nebraska Press, 2004), p. 84.

23. Tygiel, *Baseball's Great Experiment*, pp. 103–104.

24. Lamb, *Blackout*, p. 103.

25. Lamb, *Blackout*, p. 108.

26. *Philadelphia Daily News*, October 27, 1972. Cited in Rampersad, *Jackie Robinson*, p. 145.

27. Jackie Robinson, "Now I Know Why They Boo Me!" *Look*, January 15, 1955, pp. 22–28.

28. Tygiel, *Baseball's Great Experiment*, p. 116.

29. Robinson, *I Never Had It Made*, p. 46.

30. Rampersad, *Jackie Robinson*, p. 151.

31. Robinson, *I Never Had It Made*, p. 47.

32. Robinson, *I Never Had It Made*, p. 47.

33. Tygiel, *Baseball's Great Experiment*, pp. 124–125.

34. Tygiel, *Baseball's Great Experiment*, p. 141.

35. Robinson, *I Never Had It Made*, p. 51.

36. Falkner, *Great Time Coming*, p. 142; Robinson, *I Never Had It Made*, p. 52.

Chapter 5

BREAKING BARRIERS, 1947

Robinson ran from the happy mob of Montreal fans because he had to catch a plane to Detroit. He had arranged to join a barnstorming tour of the Midwest and West as soon as the Little World Series ended. The mixed-race squad included Royals teammates like Al Campanis and Marvin Rackley, as well as Negro League stars. The group played for several weeks in October and November, but an unscrupulous promoter made off with most of the money they earned. When Robinson got home to Los Angeles, he had to resort to semi-pro basketball and local speaking engagements to make some much-needed cash.

Rachel had traveled back to California alone and had settled into her mother's house to spend the final month of her pregnancy. Robinson was there with her when she went into labor on November 18. She gave birth to a healthy son, Jack Roosevelt Robinson Junior, later that day. The new family stayed with Zellee Isum for the rest of the off-season.

While the Robinsons were enjoying their little boy and adjusting to parenthood, Branch Rickey was enduring a contentious round of meetings with baseball's other owners. The proceedings of the winter meetings were private and have stayed that way, but Rickey and others have related that nearly all of the owners of the major-league baseball clubs expressed their opposition to the idea of integrating the game. According to Rickey, the owners drew up a secret report that said, in part: "However well-intentioned, the use of Negro players would hazard all the physical properties of baseball."[1] Other versions of the incident hold that the owners voted 15–1 against the inclusion of black players, with Rickey as the sole vote in favor.

At this point, Rickey had not announced any intention to bring Robinson up to the majors in the coming season. It seems clear, however, that this was his plan, because he began to quietly meet with prominent New York blacks to call for moderation if and when Robinson joined the Dodgers. "One of the greatest hazards is the overenthusiasm of some Negroes—the overexcitable ones who by very excess of pride may cause tension and clashes," he told them.[2] In Rickey's view, a too-demonstrative black community would antagonize whites and set them against Robinson. Rickey asked the group to put out the word in their churches, newspapers, and civic groups: they were not to use Robinson "as a symbol of social 'ism' or schism, a triumph of race over race," but to cheer him simply as a ballplayer.[3] Rickey's fears were deeply prejudiced, even racist in their own way, but they seem to have been shared by many of the African American leaders. Over the next few weeks and months, numerous black publications echoed Rickey's pleas for good behavior on the part of black fans.[4]

Meanwhile in the mainstream press, sportswriters debated Robinson's chances to, as they put it, "make the grade" in the major leagues. From pro-and-con columns in the *Sporting News* to polls of sportswriters and editors, Jackie Robinson was the talk of the sports world that winter.

As far as Robinson was concerned, all the chatter meant nothing. When he left Rachel and Jackie Junior in Los Angeles and set off for spring training on February 20, he was still assigned to the Royals. This made him feel impatient and anxious; all the other top International League hitters of 1946 had already been promoted to their parent teams. Robinson believed that he could trust Rickey, but the suspense was hard to bear.[5]

PLANS AND PROTESTS

The reason for the delay was that Rickey had a grand plan in mind as the final stage of his "Great Experiment," and it required Robinson to remain on the minor-league roster. Rickey had arranged for the Dodgers and Royals to work through their spring conditioning and exhibition programs away from the racism of Florida, and outside the United States entirely, in Cuba and in Panama. Both baseball-mad nations fielded teams in which race had never been an issue, and Rickey wanted to expose his players to their color-blind tolerance. Rickey's idea was that in 12 scheduled Dodger–Royal exhibition games, Robinson would perform against the Dodgers so brilliantly that they would spontaneously clamor for him to be brought up to the team. "If Robinson merits being with the Dodgers, I'd prefer to have the players want him, rather than force him on the players,"

Rickey told a reporter. "I want Robinson to have the fairest chance in the world without the slightest bit of prejudice."[6]

Leo Durocher thought this notion was nuts. Durocher, the Dodgers' scrappy and tough-talking pit bull of a manager, did not expect sweetness and brotherly love from his ballplayers. Astutely, he understood that the minor-league Royals put up no fuss against Robinson because they were not in a position to protest anything; they were happy just to have jobs. Big leaguers, with fans and influence of their own, were much less likely to meekly accept Robinson into their midst. Durocher, for his part, had seen Robinson in a few exhibition games and wanted him on the Dodgers immediately: "You could see he was a really good hitter. And that nothing in the world scared him."[7]

When the Dodgers traveled to Panama for their round of exhibition games in March, Durocher got wind of a protest arising from certain members of his team. It was rumored that a group of mostly Southern-born Dodgers was circulating an anti-Robinson petition. The protesters, or so the story went, included Dixie Walker, the popular Georgian outfielder; Kirby Higbe, a pitcher from South Carolina; Bobby Bragan, a catcher from Alabama; and Hugh Casey, a pitcher from Georgia. The upstarts were not limited to those of Southern origin: outfielder Carl Furillo, who was from Pennsylvania, was vociferously opposed to the integration of the team. At the same time, a number of southerners refused to sign, including Pete Reiser, who had run into Robinson in the service, and Pee Wee Reese, the team's shortstop and a clubhouse leader. "I just wanted to play the game," Reese said later, "and it didn't matter to me whether he was black or green, he had a right to be there, too."[8]

Durocher had no way of knowing how widespread the revolt had become. He decided to squelch it fast before he had an outright mutiny on his hands. "What did the damn fools think they were going to do—strike?" he wondered.[9] In these days before players' unions, the owners held all the power. The players couldn't possibly win a fight like this, but they could tear the team apart.

Durocher roused the men out of bed for a midnight meeting. They gathered in the largest room available, a kitchen. Durocher, in pajamas and dressing gown, proceeded to bawl the players out in his usual profane manner. "I hear some of you fellows don't want to play with Robinson and that you have a petition drawn up," he began. "Well, boys, you know what you can do with that petition. You can wipe your ass with it ... If this fellow is good enough to play on this ballclub—and from what I've seen and heard, he is—he is going to play on this ballclub and he is going to play for *me* ... This fellow is a real great ballplayer. He's going to win pennants for us. He's going to put money in your pockets and money in mine…So I don't want to see your petition and I don't want to hear anything more about it. The meeting is over; go back to bed."[10]

Rickey arrived in Panama the next day and interviewed each of the segregationist Dodgers one on one. Within a year, nearly all of them would be traded away or cut from the Brooklyn roster.

Robinson knew nothing of these undercurrents, which were kept out of the press. He was having a hard enough time working his way through his spring training regimen in Havana. When he arrived, he had been furious to find that even here in integrated Cuba, he and the Dodger system's other black players—Campanella, Newcombe, and pitcher Roy Partlow—had been segregated from their teammates. The Dodgers were staying in a plush hotel; the Royals roomed in a brand-new dormitory at a military school. But the black players were sent to a crumbling, ill-kept hotel several miles from the practice field. They were given a car and some meal money and left to fend for themselves, relying on Campanella's few words of Spanish to communicate. Years later, Robinson was still upset about the situation, especially once he realized that the segregation was not due to local laws but to Rickey's fear of any kind of racial incident in camp.[11]

Worse than the hotel was the fact that the four men had to eat in local restaurants, while the white players had kitchens and a cooking staff at their disposal. The unfamiliar food made them sick, Robinson most of all. He had to be treated for dysentery and was too weak to play in several of the Royals' exhibition games.

Just as the critical stretch of 12 Royals–Dodgers games was about to get underway, Robinson learned he was to play the series at first base. He had never been a first baseman. But if he was going to move up to the Dodgers, he had better become one: shortstop Reese and second baseman Ed Stanky were not about to step aside for him. Moreover, the hostility Rickey had been hearing around the league made him realize that putting Robinson at second, where he had played in Montreal, might put him in real danger. A second baseman is always at risk of being knocked down or spiked by running and sliding opponents. Robinson at that position could be deliberately targeted, again and again, by bigots who could claim to have simply been trying for an extra bag. It made sense, but it also made for extra work. George Sisler, the Hall of Fame first baseman who was in camp as a coach, gave Robinson a crash course in the position.

When the Royals went to Panama, Robinson did well in matches with local teams and in three games against the Dodgers. Weak from his continuing illness, he did not hit the ball with power, but he hit the ball nonetheless. In his 12 Panama games he had a .519 batting average. Many of his hits came on perfectly executed bunts that, with his speed, Robinson could beat out for singles.

But when the teams went back to Havana and played several contests there, Robinson was sick again. He missed several games and did not play well when he was in the lineup. It was becoming clear to Rickey that there would be no groundswell of support from the players, so at last he abandoned his plan and announced that Durocher would be the one to make the final decision on Robinson's call-up. The Dodgers and Royals were scheduled to play two last exhibition games at Ebbets Field in Brooklyn on April 9 and 10. Rickey sent Robinson and Campanella back to New York early, perhaps hoping that a return to familiar food and surroundings would help them recover. Rickey now imagined that Robinson would play brilliantly in Brooklyn, allowing Durocher to declare that the Royals simply had to let him go.

Once again Rickey's plan was thwarted. On the morning of April 9, baseball commissioner Happy Chandler ruled that Durocher, "as a result of the accumulation of unpleasant incidents...which the commissioner construes as detrimental to baseball," was suspended for the 1947 season.[12]

This was the climax of a long-brewing conflict. Durocher loved the high life and had a way of generating lurid headlines—that spring, for example, he had married actress Laraine Day even though her divorce from her former husband was not yet final. A regular in the New York–Hollywood social circuit, he had friends with unsavory connections to gamblers and criminals. At a hearing in March, Durocher had pointed out that the owners of other ballclubs were friendly with these very same questionable characters, but that protest did not help his case.

His plan in shambles, Rickey decided to go ahead and do what he had intended to do all along. At 3:15 P.M. during the sixth inning of the final Dodgers–Royals exhibition game, Arthur Mann, Rickey's assistant, quietly circulated a short press release: "The Brooklyn Dodgers today purchased the contract of Jackie Roosevelt Robinson from the Montreal Royals."[13]

Down on the field, unaware of the news that was sweeping though the stadium, Robinson hit into a double play. As he jogged back to the bench, he couldn't figure out why his Royals teammates were standing and cheering. As the *Pittsburgh Courier* put it, "The great American pastime has really become American at last."[14]

THE BIG LEAGUES AT LAST

Robinson headed to the Brooklyn clubhouse after the game and was given his new uniform, number 42. The next morning he signed a Dodgers contract that would pay him the league-minimum $5,000 salary for the season. Slightly dazed, he "just sorta gulped" when Clyde Sukeforth, the Dodgers' interim manager, informed him that he would be playing first base in an exhibition game against the Yankees that afternoon.[15]

These three pre-season exhibition games at Ebbets Field drew 80,000 fans, double what would be expected in any other year. Many of the additional spectators were black, news accounts noted in what would be a theme of Dodgers coverage that season. The mood was festive; street vendors sold "I'm For Robinson" buttons outside on Sullivan Place. Robinson batted in five runs in the weekend's three games on singles and sacrifice flies, and he held down first base securely.

In the Dodgers clubhouse, reactions to Robinson were restrained. A few men shook his hand in greeting, but these were mostly former Royals who had played with him the year before. The other players simply did not know how to deal with the man at the center of their club's well-publicized drama, and despite Durocher's and Rickey's lectures, many of them were still opposed to integration. Only one of them was straight-forward enough to approach Robinson and tell him so. Second baseman Eddie Stanky went to Robinson in those first few days and said, "You're on this ballclub and as far as I'm concerned that makes you one of twenty-five players on my team. But before I play with you I want you to know how I feel about it. I want you to know I don't like it. I want you to know I don't like you."

Robinson responded, "All right. That's the way I'd rather have it. Right out in the open."[16] Mindful that many of his other teammates doubtless felt the same way, Robinson kept to himself in his first weeks with the team. Reporters soon noticed. Many began to refer to him as "the loneliest man in sports."

It helped when Rachel and Jackie Junior, whom Robinson had missed terribly, flew to New York after the Yankee exhibition series had ended. There wasn't time for them to search out a permanent place to live; the first official game of the season was scheduled for the next day. They settled as best they could into a tiny Manhattan hotel room, an awkward arrangement with a five-month-old infant to care for.

Opening Day, April 15, was frigid. The Dodgers were facing the Boston Braves, who had their ace, curveball master Johnny Sain, on the mound. Robinson, batting second, had a frustrating day at the plate. He managed to reach first base on an error in the seventh inning and came around to score the winning run in a 5–3 Dodgers victory, but that was small consolation.[17] All his life Robinson had hated to lose, but this was worse. He was a man with a lot to prove, and going 0-for-3 was no way to prove it.

Rachel was in the stands with Jackie Junior cheering as best she could while juggling the needs of her baby. She had not realized that New York spring weather could be quite so cold, and her son had nothing but a light jacket to wear. Luckily, she was seated near Roy Campanella's mother-in-law, who was happy to tuck the baby in beneath her warm fur coat. Rachel sweet-talked the hot dog vendors into warming bottles for her.

In the Dodgers' next game, on April 17, Robinson notched his first major-league hit, a bunt single, and his team won again. The next day, led by their new manager Burt Shotton, the Dodgers were beaten 10–4 by their hated cross-town rivals, the New York Giants, at the Polo Grounds. Robinson hit his first big-league home run. When his first week in the majors ended, Robinson was hitting .429 and playing error-free ball at first base—not a bad start for a rookie.

"WHY DON'T YOU YELL AT SOMEBODY WHO CAN ANSWER BACK?"

It was a week-long grace period, and then some of the worst of Branch Rickey's predictions came true. The Philadelphia Phillies, led by manager Ben Chapman, came to Brooklyn for a three-game series on April 22. When Robinson headed to the plate in the bottom of the first inning, he was astounded at the cascade of vicious words that were hurled his way from the Phillies in their dugout. Years later, he could still remember their insults:

"'Hey, nigger, why don't you go back to the cotton field where you belong?'

"'They're waiting for you in the jungles, black boy!'

"'Hey, snowflake, which one of those white boys' wives are you dating tonight?'"[18]

Others recalled even worse epithets: "Chapman mentioned everything from thick lips to the supposedly extra-thick Negro skull...[and] the repulsive sores and diseases he said Robinson's teammates would become infected with if they touched the towels or combs he used," according to a Dodgers front-office man who was there.[19]

Bench jockeying—the shouting of insults and catcalls at members of the opposing team—has always been part of the game, and certainly Robinson had heard more than his share of name-calling in his short baseball career. But this torrent of hatred was on another level of cruelty, orders of magnitude beyond what he had experienced in Baltimore and Louisville.

Apparently his teammates agreed that the abuse was excessive. The Philadelphia bench kept up their taunts all through the second game of the series and into the third. However he felt about integration, that was enough for Ed Stanky. He screamed out, "Listen, you yellow-bellied cowards, why don't you yell at somebody who can answer back?"[20] The press got involved, too, pointing out Chapman's history of bigotry and ridiculing his attempt to pass the whole thing off as standard-issue bench behavior.

Rickey saw a silver lining in the hateful cloud when he observed that Chapman and his slurs "solidified and unified thirty men, not one of whom was willing to sit by and see someone kick around a man who had his hands tied behind his back."[21]

The incident rattled Robinson more than he wanted to admit. In the first Dodgers–Phillies game, he scored the winning run after he singled, stole second, and took third on an error, putting him into position to run home on a teammate's single. But that was Robinson's last hit for his next 20 at-bats. He agonized over the slump, although he was grateful for the calm patience of manager Burt Shotton and cheered by a reunion with his Army buddy Joe Louis, who came to Brooklyn to see the Dodgers play the Giants. Robinson continued to play first base throughout the drought, which he finally ended on May 1 with a line-drive home run against the Cubs.

A week after that, the *New York Herald Tribune* broke a major story: the St. Louis Cardinals had planned to strike rather than play the integrated Brooklyn Dodgers when they visited Ebbets Field on May 6, and had even talked about attempting a league-wide players' strike. According to the report, which came out after the Cards had won the Brooklyn series two games to one, rumors of the strike plot had reached the Cardinals' owner, who had gone to National League president Ford Frick. Frick had responded forcefully: "If you do this you will be suspended from the league...I do not care if half the league strikes. Those who do it will encounter quick retribution. All will be suspended and I don't care if it wrecks the National League for five years. This is the United States of America and one citizen has as much right to play as another."[22]

Many players and executives in the Cardinals organization denied the story and continued to deny it decades later. There's no doubt, however, that the uproar it caused focused even greater attention on the issue of racial discrimination. Frick's ringing defense of Robinson and the Dodgers struck a chord among Americans and began to change public opinion on segregation.

While the nation was discussing race, the center of the controversy was trying to just think baseball. On May 9, the same day the strike story broke, Robinson debuted in his first major-league game outside New York, at Shibe Park in Philadelphia. After the treatment he'd taken from the Phillies just two weeks before, he could only imagine what the catcalls would be like in their own ballpark. Gallingly, Rickey pressed Robinson to pose for an all-is-forgiven handshake photo with Ben Chapman, who had been vilified in the press for his team's behavior. Robinson doubted that this would fool anyone, but he agreed to do it "for the good of the game." Still, he would say years later, of all the indignities he endured that season, the photo shoot was one of the hardest things he had to endure.[23] When the two men posed, Chapman refused even to touch Robinson's hand. He grudgingly agreed to grasp the handle of a bat as Robinson held the barrel.

Perhaps it was good for baseball, but the photo didn't change much about the chatter from the Philadelphia bench. In this series, the players took to pointing bats at Robinson and making rat-a-tat machine-gun noises, which was charming in light of the death threats he had begun to receive. Robinson answered them the only way he could, with base hits and runs scored, as he continued what would become a 14-game hitting streak.

"To be able to hit with everybody yelling at him," Reese would marvel years later. "He had to block all that out, block everything out but this ball that is coming in at a hundred miles an hour and he's got a split second to make up his mind if it's in or out or up or down or coming at his head, a split second to swing. To do what he did has got to be the most tremendous thing I've ever seen in sports."[24]

Life on the road with the Dodgers was especially challenging, as Rickey had anticipated. While only one National League city, St. Louis, was located in the openly segregated South, racial separation was the custom in northern cities, too. But figuring out which hotels and restaurants within those cities would welcome Robinson and which would turn him away was difficult. In Philadelphia, despite their room reservations, the team was not allowed to check into its regular hotel because Robinson was with them; they all decamped to another hotel in the city, which did not object to his presence. In Cincinnati, the team hotel allowed Robinson to check in, but he could not use its restaurant or pool. In St. Louis, the boundaries were firm: Robinson had to stay in a different hotel entirely.

True to his promise to Branch Rickey, Robinson did not protest this treatment, no matter how much it hurt. Instead, he kept himself within strict self-imposed boundaries. "While traveling with the club, I was afraid to accept invitations to parties in strange towns or even to eat in a restaurant where I wasn't known," he wrote later. "I worried about getting into a situation that would result in bad publicity. I was on guard night and day."[25]

Meanwhile, Rachel had found a temporary home, a rented room in an apartment in Brooklyn's Bedford-Stuyvesant neighborhood. Many of the Dodgers had similar arrangements during the season. The room didn't give the little family much privacy, but it was an improvement over the hotel room, whose tiny dimensions had made such tasks as washing diapers, preparing formula, and bathing Jackie Junior difficult. Their new residence also gave them a chance to get to know Brooklyn better. "The feeling in Brooklyn was very supportive, very rich, and we loved it," Rachel would say later.[26]

The May road trip saw Robinson begin to come into his own as a player. By the time it ended on May 21, he and the Dodgers had faced every team in the National League. Robinson had stood up to taunts, abuse, threats, and indignities unbowed. He had been hit by pitches six times (more than had any single player in the entire 1946 season). Through it all his hitting steadily improved, reaching .283 and giving him more chances to make a difference with his agility on the basepaths. And his greatest asset of all, his phenomenal intensity and drive to win, had started to shine through. At the end of the month, with the Dodgers two games out of first place, Wendell Smith reported that "there is more warmth toward [Robinson] these days in both the dugout and the clubhouse."[27]

THE ROOKIE SETTLES IN

The Dodgers played home games for much of June, and Robinson grew into his role at Ebbets Field. Starting on June 14, he had a 21-game hitting streak that pushed his batting average up to .311; on June 24, in a 4–2 victory over the Pittsburgh Pirates, he stole home for the first time in his major-league career. It happened when the game was tied 2–2 and Robinson, at third base, saw that pitcher Fritz Ostermueller was concentrating on the batter and not the runners. Robinson began to weave and feint on and off the bag; Ostermueller ignored him, obviously dismissing his moves as nothing more than distraction tactics. On the next pitch, a ball, Robinson shot home and slid in safely with the go-ahead run. The fans roared their approval—"the best reward a player can get," Robinson would say—and his signature play was born.[28]

The Dodgers were drawing large crowds both at home and on the road from the very beginning of the season. At the time, many reporters and other observers linked these ticket sales to Robinson's presence; one postseason article asserted that "the National League intake [in 1947] was nearly a quarter of a million dollars above normal" and credited it all to Robinson.[29] Recent statistical analysis has called this into question.

Baseball attendance overall had surged in the 1946 season, and while every National League team but Philadelphia posted further gains in 1947, those ticket sales didn't come only from games played with Brooklyn. (Brooklyn itself, already the top draw in the league, had the smallest attendance increase of all.) It is probable that baseball itself was enjoying a postwar vogue that had little to do with the "Great Experiment."[30] Nonetheless, the popular perception was that Robinson was boosting attendance in Brooklyn and all around the league, and this notion helped to chip away at the other clubs' resistance to integration.

On July 5, the Cleveland Indians became the second team in major league baseball, and the first in the American League, to sign a black player. Larry Doby, a hard-hitting first baseman for the Newark Eagles, debuted with the Tribe that very afternoon. Indians owner Bill Veeck decided to take a markedly "unRickeylike" approach to integration, believing that Robinson's long minor league build-up and all its publicity had needlessly added to the pressure. Robinson, in a newspaper column that ran under his name in the *Pittsburgh Courier,* welcomed Doby and noted that with his signing, "I no longer have the feeling that if I don't make good it will kill the chances of other Negro players."[31] This was a feeling that only solidified when the St. Louis Browns added two black players to their roster later in July and when fastballer Dan Bankhead joined the Dodgers directly from the Negro Leagues on August 26 to shore up their winning, but fragile, pitching staff. Throughout the season, Doby said later, he and Robinson talked often to compare notes and share experiences.

In July the Dodgers took decisive possession of first place in the National League, at one point winning seven games in a row. Brooklyn had ended the 1946 season tied for first with the St. Louis Cardinals, and a hard-fought playoff series had cemented the rivalry between the two teams. Now the Cards vaulted over their season's miserable start and went on a tear of their own. In mid-August, when the two clubs met for a four-game series in Brooklyn, they both knew it would be a battle.

Robinson ended up taking the brunt of the Cardinals' fire, not at the plate (opponents had figured out by now how foolish it was to hit him with a pitch and give him a free base), but in the field. Playing first base, he was spiked twice by Cardinal runners. In the series opener on August 18, outfielder Joe Medwick stomped on Robinson's left foot, drawing blood. Then in the final game on August 20, Enos Slaughter slashed the back of Robinson's leg in the seventh inning while running over the bag on a ground-ball out. Robinson dropped to the dirt, and his teammates leaped to his defense. Though he was hurt "rather severely," he stayed in the game and funneled his feelings into onfield chatter directed at Dodgers pitcher

Ralph Branca, who had a no-hitter going. The two teams split the series, but in Robinson's view, Slaughter's aggression pulled the Dodgers together as a team and fueled their drive for the pennant.[32] Although the Cardinals kept things tight the rest of the way, Brooklyn clinched the league championship on September 22. In his first year of major-league ball, Jackie Robinson was going all the way to the World Series.

But first, he was going to reap a few rewards. Before the season began, Branch Rickey had decreed that no special treatment was allowed for Robinson, which meant there would be no celebratory days in his honor, no proclamations or parades, and no commercials or endorsement deals. Nothing was to detract from Robinson's baseball-playing mission. Eventually, Rickey relented on the endorsement restriction, and Robinson was free to add to his bare-bones $5,000 salary by doing ads for Borden's milk, Homogenized Bond bread, and even Old Gold cigarettes, despite the fact that he did not smoke and never had.

Now that the season was nearly over, Rickey permitted Robinson's admirers to declare "Jackie Robinson Day" at Ebbets Field. September 23 was the designated date, and more than 26,000 fans gathered to honor his incredible year. Mallie Robinson had taken her first-ever airplane trip to be there; Zellee Isum came, too, as did Rev. Karl Downs. Fans and sponsors presented a stream of gifts: a new Cadillac, a set of silverware, a television, a watch. On the newsstands that week, *Time* magazine featured Robinson on its cover. He also had been named the first-ever Rookie of the Year by the publication widely regarded as baseball's bible, *The Sporting News*. "The sociological experiment that Robinson represented, the trail-blazing he did, the barriers he broke down did not enter into the decision" to give him the honor, explained *The Sporting News*, whose editors had openly opposed baseball's integration for years. Rather, the award was made solely on the basis of "stark baseball values."[33] In other words, Robinson was Rookie of the Year because he was baseball's outstanding new player, not because he was baseball's outstanding new black player.

When the season officially ended, the statistics bore this out. Robinson batted .297 on the year, and his 29 stolen bases led the National League. He scored 125 runs, a team high and second in the league. His 31 doubles tied for the team lead with Dixie Walker, and his 12 home runs matched the number hit by Pee Wee Reese. In 46 bunt attempts, 42 were effective either as sacrifices or as hits, an excellent .913 success rate.

Impressive as the stats were, they did not—and never could—capture the essence of Robinson as a competitor. His daring on the basepaths added an element of surprise, a dash of Negro League-style speed and "trickiness," that hadn't been seen in major-league ball since the days of

Ty Cobb. And his innate drive to win made a real, yet intangible, difference on the field. Or, as Leo Durocher would say in his inimitable fashion, "This guy didn't just come to play. He came to beat ya. He came to stuff the goddamn bat right up your ass."[34]

The World Series that began on September 30 pitted the Dodgers against the New York Yankees in the first of six "Subway Series" that the two teams would play one another over the next decade. This one went the distance as the Bronx and Brooklyn rivals battled one another for seven games.

For Robinson, it was thrilling to be part of the series, though he was not a central figure in its drama. The powerful Yankees, who had dominated the American League all season and won the pennant by 12 games, were widely expected to defeat the Dodgers quickly. They took the first two games, held at Yankee Stadium, but the tenacious Dodgers had other ideas. When the series moved to Ebbets Field, the Brooklyn team clawed out a close victory in Game Three, and another in Game Four, when they were no-hit for eight innings by Yankee pitcher Floyd Bevins until Cookie Lavagetto, pinch-hitting for the Dodgers with two out in the ninth, smashed a two-run double for a victory that tied the series 2–2.

The fifth game, another Yankee win, featured an RBI from Robinson and a home run from the great Joe DiMaggio. Then Brooklyn evened things up again with an 8–6 triumph in the Bronx, "incredible as it may seem to a bewildered world at large," one reporter commented.[35] It all came down to game 7 at Yankee Stadium, when the Brooklyn pitching staff, exhausted, could do no more. The Yankees won the game 5–2 to take the unexpectedly hard-fought championship. Robinson had played solidly, batting .259 and putting his speed to good use: he had two stolen bases, he teased a Yankee pitcher into a balk, and he got into an opportune rundown that allowed a teammate to take an extra base in scoring position.

The summer of 1947 had seen, as many would soon realize, "perhaps baseball's first true modern season,"[36] and for Jackie Robinson it was only the beginning.

NOTES

1. Mann, *The Jackie Robinson Story*, p. 134.

2. Fulton Oursler, "Rookie of the Year," *Reader's Digest*, February 1948, pp. 34–38.

3. Mann, *The Jackie Robinson Story*, p. 163.

4. Bill L. Weaver, "The Black Press and the Assault on Professional Baseball's 'Color Line,' October, 1945–April, 1947," *Phylon*, Winter 1979, pp. 303–317.

5. Jackie Robinson, *I Never Had It Made* (New York: Ecco, 1995), p. 54.

6. *Pittsburgh Courier*, February 1, 1947. Cited in Arnold Rampersad, *Jackie Robinson: A Biography* (New York: Ballantine Books, 1998), p. 160.

7. Leo Durocher, *Nice Guys Finish Last* (New York: Simon and Schuster, 1975), p. 204.

8. Pee Wee Reese, "What Jackie Robinson Meant to an Old Friend," *New York Times*, July 17 1977, p. 52.

9. Durocher, *Nice Guys Finish Last*, p. 205.

10. Durocher, *Nice Guys Finish Last*, p. 205.

11. Robinson, *I Never Had It Made*, p. 55.

12. Durocher, *Nice Guys Finish Last*, p. 260.

13. *Sporting News*, April 16, 1947.

14. Weaver, "The Black Press and the Assault on Professional Baseball's 'Color Line,'" pp. 303–317.

15. *Pittsburgh Courier*, April 19, 1947. Cited in Rampersad, *Jackie Robinson*, p. 167.

16. Durocher, *Nice Guys Finish Last*, p. 206.

17. Robinson, *I Never Had It Made*, p. 57.

18. Robinson, *I Never Had It Made*, p. 58.

19. Jules Tygiel, *Baseball's Great Experiment* (New York: Oxford University Press, 1997), p. 182.

20. Robinson, *I Never Had It Made*, p. 60.

21. Tygiel, *Baseball's Great Experiment*, p. 183.

22. Stanley Woodward, "National League Averts Strike of Cardinals Against Robinson's Presence in Baseball," *New York Herald Tribune*, May 9, 1947, p. 24.

23. Robinson, *I Never Had It Made*, p. 62.

24. Roger Kahn, *The Boys of Summer* (New York: Perennial Library, 1987), p. 326.

25. Jackie Robinson, "Now I Know Why They Boo Me!" *Look*, January 15, 1955, pp. 22–28.

26. Rampersad, *Jackie Robinson*, p. 181.

27. Tygiel, *Baseball's Great Experiment*, p. 195.

28. Robinson, *I Never Had It Made*, p. 67.

29. Oursler, "Rookie of the Year," pp. 34–38.

30. Henry D. Fetter, "Robinson in 1947: Measuring an Uncertain Impact," in *Jackie Robinson: Race, Sports, and the American Dream* (Armonk, NY: M.E. Sharpe, 1998), pp. 183–192.

31. *Pittsburgh Courier*, July 19, 1947. Cited in Tygiel, *Baseball's Great Experiment*, p. 217.

32. Robinson, *I Never Had It Made*, pp. 67–68.

33. "Robinson 'Rookie of Year'," *New York Times*, September 13, 1947, p. 15.

34. Kahn, *The Boys of Summer*, p. 393.

35. John Drebinger, "Dodgers Set Back Yankees By 8 to 6 For 3-3 Series Tie," *New York Times*, October 6, 1947, p. 1.

36. Pete Palmer and Gary Gillette, *The Baseball Encyclopedia* (New York: Barnes and Noble Books, 2004), p. 1494.

Jackie Robinson in flight as a UCLA broad jumper, 1940. "You really try to jump off the earth," he wrote, "and your legs churn the air like you wanted to reach the moon." National Baseball Hall of Fame Library.

Robinson enters the Brooklyn Dodgers clubhouse for the first time, April 9, 1947. The Pittsburgh Courier captioned this photo: "The keep out sign doesn't mean Jackie, or any other colored player who can make the grade. The great American pastime has really become American at last." National Baseball Hall of Fame Library.

Robinson was intensely focused at the plate, as he was in every other aspect of the game. National Baseball Hall of Fame Library.

Large for a second baseman, Robinson used his size to his advantage. He would practically dare opposing baserunners to bowl him over. National Baseball Hall of Fame Library.

On the day he is inducted into the National Baseball Hall of Fame, Robinson poses with the two people he deemed most responsible for his success: Branch Rickey and Rachel Robinson. National Baseball Hall of Fame Library.

Chapter 6

THE JACKIE ROBINSON
DODGERS, 1948–1951

The Series over, Robinson headed into the off season with one objective in mind—to make some money. He would turn 29 during the winter, and he feared that his age would soon catch up with him and end his career on the field. "I've got to make it quick," he declared, if only to be able to provide for his young son's future.[1]

To that end, he launched into a four-week vaudeville tour that put him on stage in various cities to answer pre-set questions about his baseball experiences. He signed a contract to produce an autobiography with Wendell Smith and made a deal to star in a movie (this project soon fell through). He took a break for the Christmas holidays to spend some time with his family and to undergo an operation on his troublesome right ankle, but then he hit the road again, this time on a speaking tour of the South.

These ventures did put some cash in Robinson's pocket—he made far more from them than the Dodgers had paid him for his work on the ball field and more than the $12,500 1948 contract he signed in February. But there was one major drawback: they kept him from doing any kind of athletic conditioning. With all the celebrations, testimonial dinners, and charity fundraisers he was asked to attend, Robinson got out of playing shape quickly. By the time he reported to spring training, he was at least 30 pounds overweight.

Leo Durocher, suspension ended, was back at the helm as Dodgers manager. Never a calm man, he went ballistic when he saw Robinson. "What in the world happened to you? You look like an old woman!" he screamed.[2] Durocher was humiliated that the team had gone all the way to the World Series without him, so he was eager to assert his authority. He rode Robinson mercilessly all through training camp.

While Robinson recognized the seriousness of his weight problem, he bristled at Durocher's constant harping. He was preoccupied by the emotional fallout of another sudden death, that of his friend and mentor Rev. Karl Downs. Downs, plagued with chronic stomach pain, had undergone an operation near his home in Austin, Texas. He was sent to a short-staffed segregated ward for recovery, and then post-operative complications set in. The lack of quick emergency attention killed him. He was only 35.[3] Downs' death weighed on Robinson much as Frank's passing had done nine years earlier.

At the same time, it was imperative for the team that Robinson get into playing shape fast. On March 6, the Dodgers traded second baseman Ed Stanky to the Boston Braves. It was a move meant to clear the position for Robinson to play in his accustomed spot, and Robinson would need every bit of his old speed and agility to take advantage of it. Stanky had been a favorite of Durocher's, who argued long and hard against his trade. The idea of a "hog fat"—in his words—Jackie Robinson taking Stanky's spot galled him.[4]

The Dodgers' conditioning camp was held in the Dominican Republic, and in the tropical heat Robinson dropped much of his excess weight. But the dieting left him weak and powerless at the plate. The newspapers back in New York were filled with stories about his girth. At least he and Dan Bankhead were able to stay in the same quarters as the rest of the team this year; no more segregated hotels.

The preseason exhibition schedule, however, was another story. Rickey had arranged many of the Dodgers' spring games to take place in segregated southern cities like Fort Worth, Texas and Tulsa, Oklahoma. Once again Robinson was required to stay in private homes or second-rate hotels, and he struggled in the games. What with his weight-loss regimen and the spring-training travel, Robinson had had precious little time to practice with Pee Wee Reese the all-important double-play combination, a move that requires precision teamwork and timing between shortstop and second baseman. As a result, he looked awkward and hesitant in the position that he had played so brilliantly for Montreal just two years before.

In April the Dodgers returned to Brooklyn and the beginning of the 1948 season. Rachel and Jackie Junior were already there. They had driven cross-country and settled into a comfortable two-bedroom apartment at 5224 Tilden Avenue in Flatbush, Brooklyn. The neighborhood was largely Jewish and made up of small one- and two-family houses. Some of the residents had been upset by the arrival of a black homeowner, the Robinsons' landlady and downstairs neighbor, but others were welcoming. The family living two doors down, the Satlows, were particularly warm toward the Robinsons. Their youngest child and Jackie Junior were about the same age, and Rachel and Sarah Satlow forged a lifelong friendship.

ROBINSON'S SOPHOMORE SEASON

The Dodgers opened the season with a 7–6 win against the New York Giants at the Polo Grounds. Overall, though, the National League champions were ragged in the field and inconsistent at the plate, and they could do no better than a 5–5 record in their first 10 games. None of them seemed less comfortable than Robinson. His right arm was sore, his back ached, and he was still carrying 5 or 10 extra pounds. The whispers around the league began—maybe Robinson was just a one-season wonder, a flash in the pan. Finally, Durocher benched him.

Whether the time off gave his arm a rest or fired up his competitive nature, Robinson responded in the next few games with RBI and his first home run of the season. He still looked awkward in the infield, though, and Durocher tried switching him back to first base. By the end of the month, the team had endured an eight-game losing streak and had sunk all the way down to last place in the standings. Robinson's batting was back to form, with his average up around the .300 mark, but he had no successful steals.

The baseball world buzzed when Rickey put Robinson on waivers in June, a move that made him potentially available to other teams. It came as a shock to the ballplayer. Much later, Rickey claimed that he used the waiver maneuver to give Robinson some competitive motivation; he may also have been trying to gauge the other teams' trading needs or their openness to integration. Whatever Rickey's motives, for Robinson it was the low point of the "grim" beginning to his season.[5]

Through it all, the racial catcalls and taunts from opponents' benches, and from opposing fans as well, had not decreased. With Robinson's move to the middle infield, the abusers took another turn, insulting the Kentucky-born Reese for working so closely with a black man. "They were calling him some very vile names," Robinson said, "and every one bounced off of Pee Wee and hit me like a machine-gun bullet."[6]

"In our first game at Boston [on April 26] the Braves tried to give us a real bad time," Robinson wrote a few years later. "But Pee Wee shut them up. He walked over to me, put his arm around me and talked to me in a warm and friendly way, smiling and laughing. His sincerity startled the Braves, and there was no more trouble after that from them. Later, he did the same for me in other ball parks."[7]

Reese's gesture of team spirit and racial equality would one day become immortalized in children's books and ballpark statues. At the time, though, it said more about the relationship that was developing between the two men as they worked together. Over the 1948 season, they grew into one of the all-time great double-play combinations, "a thing of specialized beauty," according to a contemporary observer. "Each man has a thorough, subtle knowledge of the other's speed, range and throwing habits in the field . . . As a result of Reese's study of Robinson, and Robinson's study of Reese, the two have become the swiftest pivot men in their league."[8]

As June drew to a close, Robinson began to show signs of his old fire at the plate and on the basepaths. On June 24 in the first half of a doubleheader, he galvanized the Ebbets Field faithful with a two-out, bottom-of-the-ninth grand slam that won the ballgame. In the second game that day, he finally stole a base. A few days later he stole home and then ripped off an inside-the-park home run.

Adding to the fans' excitement, on July 1 catcher Roy Campanella was called up to Brooklyn for good, after playing a few Dodgers games in the outfield in April and then spending several weeks with the team's St. Paul affiliate to integrate the American Association circuit. (Yet another aspect of Rickey's "Great Experiment," the gradual integration of the minor leagues, was still ongoing.) Campanella, who had spent a season at double-A Nashua and another at triple-A Montreal, was more than ready: A Negro Leagues star for the Baltimore Elite Giants as a teenager, he had been playing professional ball for a decade. Now 26 and widely hailed as the best defensive catcher in all of baseball, he was coming into his own as a power hitter. In his first at-bat as a Dodger catcher, Campanella smashed a double and added two singles besides. Though the game was a 6–4 loss for the Dodgers, it was a win for Durocher, who had been agitating for Campanella's call-up for weeks.

This was one of the few wins the manager would have within the Dodger organization that season. Rickey and Durocher had been at loggerheads ever since the Stanky trade in March. It seemed to be only a matter of time before Durocher would be out of the manager's job.

Robinson's reawakening and Campanella's addition were turning points for the team that was in last place on July 2. The Dodgers improved sharply after that, and in July they began to scratch and claw their way up in the standings. Not only did the team's hitting improve, the infield settled into a groove as well. With Campanella behind the plate, young

Gil Hodges was freed from catching duties and was allowed to shine at first, and Robinson could take second base without any hovering doubts.

In the midst of the team's 21–10 run that month, Durocher was released from his contract with Brooklyn and went directly across the East River to manage the New York Giants. It was a move that outraged loyal fans of both teams, for whom the words "Brooklyn" and "Durocher" were synonymous. Once again, Burt Shotton stepped into Durocher's managerial shoes—though not his uniform; Shotton was the last major-league manager allowed to work in street clothes, rather than in the team's flannels. Although Robinson praised Durocher in the column that he contributed to the *Pittsburgh Courier*, the two would continue to clash on the field for years to come.

In August and September the Dodgers alternately surged and receded, making runs at first place and then falling back. At the center of the attack was Robinson. On August 22 he spearheaded a rare triple steal against the Boston Braves, who were making their own run at the pennant. On August 29 he hit for the cycle, notching a single, a double, a triple, and a home run in a game that put the Dodgers on top of the league. Robinson had another milestone this month, too: On August 24 he was thrown out of a ballgame for protesting an umpire's call too forcefully. The incident, something that would have irritated or angered most ballplayers, felt like a landmark moment to Robinson: the umpire wasn't singling him out on account of race, "but was treating me exactly as he would treat any ball-player who got on his nerves."[9]

In September, Boston's push was too much for the Dodgers, and they finished third behind the Braves and the Cardinals. Robinson's sophomore season was not quite what his rookie year had been, but his strong second half gave him decent numbers overall: a .296 batting average, 108 runs scored, 22 stolen bases, and 38 doubles.

In an effort to remain active in the off season *and* make extra money, Robinson took a barnstorming tour with Campanella once the regular season ended. They wrapped up the tour in California with a game against an all-star team led by Satchel Paige, who had finally gotten his major-league chance during the 1948 season with the Cleveland Indians. A few weeks later Robinson and Campanella returned to New York and took jobs as youth sports directors at the Harlem YMCA, which at the time was the social and political nerve center for the city's black community. Both men enjoyed working with kids, and they would continue their associations with the YMCA for years to come. For Robinson, however, the Y also opened a door to the emerging Civil Rights Movement. Politics would soon become increasingly important to him.

AN MVP YEAR

All the physical activity that fall and winter made a difference: Robinson arrived at spring training fit and ready to play. Mentally, he was ready too—ready to do something he had held himself back from doing for most of the past three seasons in organized baseball. He was ready to fight back.

It had been terribly hard for Robinson to keep his emotions in check, though he had tried to remain in line with Rickey's 1945 edict, to be "a man with guts enough not to fight back." He had never forgotten Rickey's warning that "one wrong move on my part would not only finish the chance for all Negroes in baseball, but it would set the cause of the Negro in America back 20 years." For Robinson, that meant "I had to keep my mouth shut and take it. I couldn't protest to an umpire and I couldn't get back a player who taunted and insulted me with racial remarks."[10]

Toward the end of the 1948 season, when Robinson joined his teammates in shouting at umpires and jawing at opposing teams, he was feeling his virtual leash slip off. This year, he made a conscious decision to compete as he had done before—fiercely and with fire. "They'd better be rough on me this year," he told a reporter, "because I'm sure going to be rough on them."[11] Within a few years he became known as one of the loudest bench jockeys and most fervent call-arguers in the league.

It was a role that seemed to make many Robinson supporters uncomfortable. "As long as I appeared to ignore insult and injury," he wrote later, "I was a martyred hero...but the minute I began to answer, to argue, to protest...I became a swellhead, a wise guy, an 'uppity' nigger." Robinson would often point out that throughout baseball history, white players who jawed at umpires and played each game with ferocity—players like Ty Cobb, Frankie Frisch, and Leo Durocher—were praised for their competitive spirit. The double standard infuriated him.[12]

Spring training took place in the Dodgers' new facility in Vero Beach, Florida, built on the site of an old military base. It was a protected and safe haven that allowed the Dodgers' black players and prospects to mingle as teammates. It was also large enough for families to join the players in camp. This year, Rachel and Jackie Junior came along to spring training. The little boy enjoyed the camp thoroughly, but Rachel was upset at the segregation her son was exposed to whenever they left the Dodger compound.

Robinson and the Dodgers started the season with a boom on Opening Day in a game against the Giants at Ebbets Field. Robinson, Campanella, and Carl Furillo all slammed home runs in the 10–3 victory. After that, though, Robinson's bat quieted. His batting average sank to a lowly .200 in the first two weeks of the season.

He turned things around quickly, though, when Shotton reshuffled the lineup to bat Robinson fourth, in the cleanup spot. In that position Robinson's fierceness was put to its best possible use. If any teammate got on base before him, it was Robinson's responsibility to move him along or bat him home. And if the first three hitters failed, Robinson's speed made him an excellent leadoff hitter for the Dodgers' next inning. Robinson, who as Durocher had known "came to beat ya" every day, shone in his new role. He hit at a resounding .400 clip all through May with 38 RBI. His play, along with excellent pitching from new Dodger callup Don Newcombe and veteran Preacher Roe, drove the Dodgers into first place.

Robinson's play was so outstanding that for the first time he led in the fan voting for the All-Star team, and he became the National League's starting second baseman—the first black All-Star in the contest's history. Six Dodgers took part in the 1949 matchup at Ebbets Field, including Campanella and Newcombe. When Cleveland's Larry Doby came into the game as a replacement, the historic moment was complete: Both the National and the American Leagues had broken the color barrier in All-Star play. Robinson hit a double in the 11–7 American League win, which despite the score felt like a victory for him. He had been recognized by the fans on his own terms.

A few days later Robinson took a tentative step into national politics when he testified before a congressional committee in Washington, DC. By now he had become widely regarded as a spokesman for his race, though he himself would emphasize that "I don't think I can speak for the 15 million Negroes in the country."[13] But neither, he believed, could Paul Robeson, the influential singer and actor.

Robeson was a passionate advocate for racial equality and civil rights, and he had expressed his sympathies with socialist ideas and the Communist Party. In the late 1940s it was dangerous to be associated with anything even hinting at "red" tendencies. It was the beginning of the Cold War and the Soviet Union was the enemy, as far as most Americans were concerned.

The House Un-American Activities Committee, or HUAC, had been formed to root out communism in American society. Robeson was a particular target of the committee after he made a speech in which he said it was "unthinkable" that American blacks "would go to war on behalf of those who have oppressed us for generations" to fight the Soviet Union, which in his view treated people of color with dignity.[14]

The line caused an uproar, and Robinson was asked to refute it under oath. He agonized over whether to appear before the committee, which was already sowing seeds of suspicion and fear throughout the country. He consulted with Branch Rickey, a forceful anti-Communist who was in favor of Robinson testifying; with Rachel, who urged caution; and with an NAACP representative, who counseled against testifying. Finally he decided to appear, because, as he said later, "I was black and [Robeson] wasn't speaking for me."[15] Robinson was proud of having served in the armed forces, despite all his problems there, and he believed that blacks would again fight to defend the country if necessary.

Robinson gave his statement to the committee on July 18. While criticizing Robeson's assertion and condemning communism, he took the opportunity to denounce racism, segregation, and Jim Crow in a short speech that came across as strongly patriotic. His appearance was front-page news nationwide, though the mainstream press largely ignored the anti-racism aspect of his message. Years later Robinson was still unsure if he had made the right decision.

That summer, though, it seemed that Robinson could do no wrong. He returned to the Dodgers the same day and resumed his hitting spree. At the end of July his batting average reached .364 and led the National League. And in August the song "Did You See Jackie Robinson Hit That Ball?" rose to number 13 on the pop charts, a sure measure of his national stature and popularity.

On September 20, as the season drew to a close, Robinson stole home in a victory over the Chicago Cubs. It was his fifth steal of home, now his trademark play, in the season. When it all wrapped up, Robinson, who had appeared in every one of the Dodgers' games, led the league in hitting with a .342 average; he had 37 stolen bases, the best in the majors. His position as the cleanup hitter paid off with 124 RBI, second-best in the National League. He scored runs too—122 of them. (The Dodgers as a team scored a league-leading 879 runs; Robinson was responsible for more than a quarter of that total.) Best of all, his sterling performance helped keep the Dodgers in first or second place in the standings all through August and September. They were just a half-game up on the St. Louis Cardinals on the last day of the season, but they hung on to win a thrilling 10-inning game in Philadelphia and take the National League pennant.

Then it was back to the Bronx for another installment of the Dodgers–Yankees postseason drama. The powerhouse Bombers, driven by their fine pitching staff and especially reliever Joe Page, had pulled through a tight race of their own to grab the pennant from the Boston Red

Sox. The two World Series combatants had identical 97–57 records, and most observers gave Brooklyn, with their seemingly unstoppable offense, the edge.

But as they say, "good pitching beats good hitting," and that was never more true than in the 1949 World Series. Everything the Dodgers did well, the Yankees seemed to do just a bit better. Don Newcombe's five-hitter in Game One was outdone by Allie Reynolds, who held the Brooklyn bats to two hits and took a 1–0 victory. The Dodgers won just one game, Game Two, but the Yankees took the final three games of the series, and the championship, with little difficulty. Their pitching effectively silenced Robinson, who scratched out just three hits and four walks over the five games and didn't steal a single base.

Still, much of the credit for Brooklyn's single victory in the series had to be given to Robinson. While Brooklyn's Preacher Roe pitched a 1–0 shutout, the Yankees' Vic Raschi threw a great game, too—except for the second inning, when Robinson belted a double. Once he was on base, he feinted and dodged toward third, drawing throws from the mound and rattling the Yankees thoroughly. Raschi said later, "Robinson had broken my concentration. I was pitching more to Robinson than I was to [Gil] Hodges and as a result I threw one up into Gil's power and he got the base hit that beat me."[16]

When the season ended, Dodgers earned two of baseball's major honors. Pitcher Don Newcombe, Brooklyn's latest black star, was named Rookie of the Year. His 149 strikeouts, second in the league, heralded the arrival of a major fastball talent. And on November 18, Robinson was voted the National League's Most Valuable Player (MVP). He called it "the nicest thing that could have happened to me."[17]

NEW HORIZONS

Robinson took a postseason barnstorming tour once again, this time leading a team billed as the Jackie Robinson All-Stars that included Campanella, Newcombe, and Larry Doby. When it was cut short by injuries to several of the players, he returned to New York, where Rachel was settling into their new home, a house they had purchased in the mixed-race neighborhood of St. Albans, Queens. Robinson planned to do some painting and refurbishing himself as Rachel rested. She was in the final weeks of her second pregnancy.

In between home-repair tasks, Robinson took on some very visible projects that kept him in the public eye: a twice-weekly sports television show, a daily radio program, and a movie deal. This film would be a biographical account called "The Jackie Robinson Story" in which Robinson would play himself. Soon after Rachel gave birth to baby Sharon on January 13—and just after he negotiated a new $35,000 contract for the 1950 season—the proud new father headed out to Hollywood for the one-month movie shoot.

Robinson had never acted, but he worked hard to learn his lines and relax in front of the camera. He insisted on including Kenny Washington and other Pasadena and UCLA teammates in the film. The script, which had been carefully vetted by Rickey and his staff, was an accurate if burnished reflection of Robinson's early years, his Negro League and minor league experiences, and his first season with the Dodgers, ending on a patriotic note with his HUAC testimony.

The moviemaking process was repetitive and somewhat exasperating. "The way they had me running bases, stealing second, running from first to third over and over again—I never had any spring training in which I worked any harder," Robinson told a reporter.[18]

Things got easier for him when he sent for Rachel and Sharon about a week into the shoot. Ruby Dee, the actress who played Rachel in the film, was thrilled to cuddle with the three-week-old Sharon and deeply impressed by her real-life counterpart. Dee said later that as soon as she met Rachel, "I had the feeling I wasn't doing her justice…She was a stronger woman than I portrayed."[19]

The shoot ended in time for Robinson to make it to spring training in Vero Beach as scheduled. A few weeks later, on May 16, the film opened in New York. It had been a low-budget production, and it showed. But critics almost universally praised Robinson's performance for his dignity, composure, and sympathy. The movie did good business, especially in small cities and towns where people had not had the chance to see the national phenomenon, Jackie Robinson, in action. It remains a fascinating peek at Robinson in his prime.

"THE INDISPENSABLE MAN"

Meanwhile, on real-life ball fields Robinson was tearing up the league once more. An ankle sprain he suffered in spring training slowed him down on the basepaths, though he remained a threat to steal, but at the plate he was as fearsome as ever. He had one of the best starts of his career in terms of hitting: at the beginning of July he was batting .371 with 53 RBI. Brooklyn stayed on top of the standings through May and June on the strength of their hard-hitting lineup, which included power hitters like Hodges, Campanella, and center fielder Duke Snider, as well as those who hit for average like Robinson and Carl Furillo. The National League champions were confident they could take the pennant again.

On July 2, Robinson had perhaps his worst on-field blowup against an umpire yet. Stalking away from the plate and muttering about a called third strike in a game against Philadelphia, umpire Jocko Conlan taunted him: "That strike was right down the middle." Robinson turned back, amazed and angry, and Conlan repeated his statement. When Robinson began to shout at him, Conlan tossed him from the game. Robinson had no doubt umpires were deliberately making calls against him, and many of the other Dodgers agreed.[20]

For the second year in a row, Robinson was voted into the All-Star lineup. The game was an exciting 14-inning affair that the National League won 4–3. Robinson hit a single in the second inning and came around to score the Nationals' first run when Enos Slaughter lashed a triple into the depths of Chicago's Comiskey Park.

After the All-Star break, however, the Dodgers began to falter. Their pitching staff was thin, and relievers blew leads time and again. Turmoil in the front office may have been having some effects, too. The sudden death of one of the team's co-owners led to a noisy battle for control, with Branch Rickey pitted against Walter O'Malley. Rickey, as general manager, had had the most to do with player relations and the day-to-day operation of the club. Many of the players felt some loyalty to him, Robinson perhaps most of all. But as the season wore on, O'Malley bought control of additional shares in the team and muscled Rickey aside. Robinson knew well how O'Malley felt about him ("Rickey's prima donna" had been one of the kinder things the part-owner had called the second baseman); on August 12, he told a newspaperman, "It wouldn't surprise me if I were traded."[21]

Robinson's performance had slid along with the club's. In August, his batting average was a paltry .118 in the worst slump of his major-league career. A string of nagging injuries plagued him and took him out of the lineup several times.

Brooklyn managed to make the season into a real race at the end of September. They trailed the Philadelphia Phillies by nine games as late as September 18, but in the final two weeks of play, they charged, winning 13 of 16 games. It was an impressive drive, but it was not enough. In true Hollywood style, the final game of the season was between Brooklyn and Philadelphia at Ebbets Field. A Brooklyn win would tie the season and force a playoff. The game went into extra innings, but the Phillies won it 4–1 when Dick Sisler hit a three-run homer in the tenth inning. (The Yankees would beat them in four straight games in the World Series.)

It was Robinson's intensity that drove the team when it was winning. As Dodger coach Jake Pitler put it, "He's the indispensable man. When he hits we win. When he doesn't, we just don't look the same."[22] In spite of his miserable August, he batted .328 overall, second in the league behind Stan Musial, and he seemed to be perpetually on base with 80 walks on top of his 170 hits. What's more, it seemed his style of play—aggressive baserunning, high-average batting with power—had permeated the club. Brooklyn led the league in hits, runs scored, batting average, and stolen bases. By the end of the 1950s, the entire National League would strive to combine speed and power, Negro League-style. Robinsons's innovations heralded what one analyst has called the "third age of modern baseball."[23]

His stats were little consolation to Robinson. The close pennant loss depressed him, and O'Malley's ascendance worried him. Rickey lost his general manager's job when he announced on October 28 that O'Malley had bought him out to become majority owner of the Dodgers. O'Malley "seemed to become furious" if Branch Rickey's very name was mentioned in conversation, Robinson would recall. The team's new owner was well aware of the bond that Robinson had established with Rickey, and as Robinson understood it, that made him "the target of [O'Malley's] insecurity."[24] The two men would clash both publicly and privately for the next six years.

UNDER NEW MANAGEMENT

The 1951 season was a heartbreaking one for Brooklyn fans. The Dodgers led the league for most of the season until an amazing stretch run by another team snatched the pennant from their hands. Brooklyn out-hit, out-ran, and out-powered every other team in the league, but somehow the New York Giants came back to tie the season on the last day to force a three-game playoff and—for them—a miraculous close.

O'Malley asserted his authority quickly by firing Burt Shotton and bringing in Chuck Dressen to manage the club. Otherwise, the 1951 Dodgers were more or less the same team that had taken the field in 1950. Despite Robinson's concerns, O'Malley made no move to trade him. In the off-season, after completing his customary barnstorming tour, he signed a new contract for $39,750.

Spring training went smoothly until an O'Malley innovation caused problems for Robinson and for Brooklyn's other black players. O'Malley decided that while the conditioning part of the program would take place at the Vero Beach compound, the Dodgers would be based in segregated Miami for their exhibition games. The black players and their families could not live in the same hotel as the other Dodgers, ride the same buses, or even catch taxicabs. Rachel, who with Jackie Junior and Sharon accompanied her husband in Florida, found that the situation set her apart from the other team wives in a way that would affect their relationships for the rest of the season.

When the season began, the Dodgers got off to a solid start. Their starting pitchers were strong enough to offset the still-suspect bullpen: Preacher Roe would win 22 games, and Don Newcombe would strike out 164 men, tying Boston's Warren Spahn for the lead in that category. The hitters kept up their pace from the previous season: in early June, Robinson was batting .412 and the rest of the lineup was productive as well. Injury-free, Robinson was running the bases like he used to and worrying his opponents' pitching in the process. Brooklyn took the lead in the standings early and didn't look likely to loosen its grip.

It infuriated Leo Durocher, whose Giants had been predicted to win the pennant. The two New York teams met for six games in April, and the Dodgers took five games out of the six as insults and beanballs flew. Throughout, Robinson and Durocher were verbally at one another's throats. Durocher would deride Robinson as big-headed; Robinson would suggest that Durocher was wearing his wife's perfume. It was a display of machismo that had an element of the schoolyard to it, too. Much later, both men would say that their competitive natures made them simply too much alike.[25]

Ballfield posturing was one thing, but threats of violence were another, and Robinson was still being subjected to those. On May 20, Brooklyn was scheduled to play a game at Cincinnati's Crosley Field when the Reds received a letter containing a death threat against Robinson. The anonymous writer was chillingly specific: While Robinson was on the baseball field, a sniper would shoot him from the rooftop of a nearby building. Told of the threat, the team reacted with gallows humor: "I think we will all wear 42, and then they will have a shooting gallery," Reese suggested. "You would have to darken up, too," noted Robinson.[26]

Police officers swept the roofs and were out in force around the ballpark, and nothing came of the threat other than the Dodgers' reaction to it: they scored 24 runs, including a two-run homer by Robinson, to sweep a doubleheader.

Robinson went to the 1951 All-Star Game on the strength of his popularity in the fan balloting, and six other Dodgers joined him in Detroit's Briggs Stadium. The National League won the game 8–3, and

Robinson earned an RBI when he dropped a precisely placed bunt down the third-base line, allowing the Phillies' Richie Ashburn to score from third.

By August 12, Brooklyn looked to be running away with the pennant, with 13-½ games between them and the second-place Giants. But the New York team refused to give up, and the Dodgers began to stumble. They were swept in a three-game series at the Polo Grounds as the Giants put together a 16-game winning streak. After the two clubs met again in early September, the Brooklyn lead in the standings was whittled down to five. They were not collapsing by any means—they had a .600 winning percentage in the season's second half—but the Giants were on a roll that has rarely been equaled in baseball history, capped by a seven-game winning streak at the end of the season. On the last day the two teams were tied, each with 95 wins and 58 losses.

The Giants were scheduled to play in Boston that day; the Dodgers, in Philadelphia. The New Yorkers quickly dispatched the Braves 3–2 and then tuned in the clubhouse radio to keep tabs on the only other game that mattered. Preacher Roe, pitching on two days' rest, had given up four runs to the Phillies and was replaced by Ralph Branca, who gave up two more. Brooklyn fought back with a string of hits, including a two-run triple by Robinson, and Philadelphia responded. In the ninth inning the score was tied 8–8.

With two outs and the bases loaded in the twelfth inning, Phillies first baseman Eddie Waitkus slammed a Don Newcombe fastball up the middle of the field. A hit would end the game and the Brooklyn season. The shot looked uncatchable, but Robinson launched his body at the ball, speared it, and hit the ground hard. Winded, he passed out briefly and stayed down for several long minutes. "Rachel started to cry when she saw me from the stands," Robinson wrote later. "She was sure I was dead."[27] But he held on to the ball for the out, getting Newcombe out of the jam and keeping the Dodgers alive.

"I would have quit the game if it hadn't been for Pee Wee [Reese,]" Robinson remembered a few months afterward. "He talked to me and kidded me and pulled me together."[28] In the fourteenth inning Robinson came to the plate against Phillies ace Robin Roberts and connected with a 1–1 fastball that sailed into Shibe Park's left-field upper deck. It was the winning hit of the 9–8 game, and the Dodgers and Giants were still tied for the National League pennant.

Under league rules that meant a three-game playoff series would decide the championship. With the World Series set to begin on October 4, the playoff had to begin the very next day. The two teams, exhausted, headed to Ebbets Field.

The first game was won by the Giants, 3–2, in a home run derby in which all the scoring came on long balls hit by New York's Bobby Thomson and Monte Irvin and Brooklyn's Andy Pafko. Game Two at the Polo Grounds was a Dodgers laugher that they won 10–0. It all came down to Game Three, again set for the old Manhattan ballpark.

The pitching matchup was fastballer versus fastballer, the Giants' Sal Maglie against the Dodgers' Don Newcombe. A first-inning single by Robinson yielded a run, and the score stayed 1–0 until the seventh, when Irvin scored on a Thomson sacrifice. A series of Dodger singles and sacrifices and Giant misplays brought the score to 4–1 in the eighth, and it looked as if Brooklyn might pull out a win.

In the bottom of the ninth, with Newcombe still on the mound, the Giants chipped away. Two singles and a double made the score 4–2. With Bobby Thomson coming to bat and the rookie phenomenon Willie Mays on deck, Dressen pulled the laboring Newcombe out of the game. In his place, he sent Ralph Branca to the mound.

It was a move that baseball fans have second-guessed ever since: Branca had pitched eight full innings just two days before, during which Thomson had touched him for a home run. Branca's first pitch was a strike. His second sailed over the left-field wall and into the hysterical crowd for a three-run bomb, and the game, and the season. Radio announcer Russ Hodges' cries of "The Giants win the pennant! The Giants win the pennant!" captured the stunning moment.

As a jubilant Thomson rounded the bases and fans rushed the field, the disconsolate Dodgers trudged across the ballpark to their center-field clubhouse. Only one man remained at his post. Robinson followed Thomson around the bases with his eyes to be sure that he touched every bag. Later, he was the only Brooklyn player to visit the New York clubhouse and congratulate the winners.

When it was all over, Campanella was named the league's MVP on the strength of his 33 home runs, 33 doubles, .325 batting average, and outstanding work behind the plate. Robinson had a fine year, too, one he considered to be his best yet. He finished among the top five in six offensive categories: batting average, on-base percentage, runs scored, hits, doubles, and stolen bases.

In these first years after the initial shock of Jackie Robinson's arrival in major-league baseball, his grittiness and zeal to win shaped the team that coalesced around him, just as much as his aggressive baserunning and tough at-bats shaped their games. The "Jackie Robinson Dodgers," as sportswriter Roger Kahn would call them, were "outspoken, opinionated, bigoted, tolerant, black, white, open, passionate: in short, a fascinating mix of vigorous men."[29]

At the same time, Kahn pointed out, Robinson changed baseball fans as well. "By applauding Robinson, a man did not feel that he was taking a stand on school integration, or on open housing. But for an instant he had accepted Robinson simply as a hometown ball player. To disregard color, even for an instant, is to step away from the old prejudices, the old hatred. That is not a path on which many double back."[30] For the ballplayer at the center of it all, and for the nation too, the only way was forward.

NOTES

1. Arnold Rampersad, *Jackie Robinson: A Biography* (New York: Ballantine Books, 1998), p. 189.

2. *Pittsburgh Courier*, March 13, 1948. Cited in Rampersad, *Jackie Robinson*, p. 94.

3. Jackie Robinson, *I Never Had It Made* (New York: Ecco, 1995), p. 70.

4. Leo Durocher, *Nice Guys Finish Last* (New York: Simon and Schuster, 1975), p. 276.

5. Robinson, *I Never Had It Made*, p. 72.

6. Jackie Robinson as told to Ed Reid, "Robinson's Team Stands By Him," *Washington Post*, August 28, 1949, p. C1.

7. Jackie Robinson, "A Kentucky Colonel Kept Me in Baseball," *Look*, February 8 1955, pp. 82–90. There is no photograph of Reese's gesture, and no contemporary newspaper accounts mentioned it. Later, Reese himself placed the incident in Cincinnati's Crosley Field and was not sure if it occurred in 1947 or 1948. Robinson's earliest so-called autobiography, which was actually written by Wendell Smith and published in 1948, does not mention it at all; his 1949 newspaper series does.

8. John Lardner, "Reese and Robinson: Team Within a Team," *New York Times Magazine*, September 9, 1949, pp. 17–19.

9. Robinson, *I Never Had It Made*, p. 75.

10. Jackie Robinson, "Now I Know Why They Boo Me!" *Look*, January 15, 1955, pp. 22–28.

11. Glenn Stout and Dick Johnson, *Jackie Robinson: Between the Baselines* (San Francisco: Woodford Press, 1997), p. 111.

12. Robinson, *I Never Had It Made*, p. 79. In this autobiography Robinson says that Rickey verbally released him from his nonconfrontation pledge before the season began, but several other sources maintain that the change was a mutual agreement.

13. Jackie Robinson as told to Ed Reid, "Robeson Has Wrong Outlook," *Washington Post*, August 30, 1949, p. 14.

14. *New York Times*, April 21, 1949.

15. Robinson, *I Never Had It Made*, p. 83.

16. Jules Tygiel, *Baseball's Great Experiment* (New York: Oxford University Press, 1997), p. 191.

17. *Pittsburgh Courier*, November 26, 1949. Cited in Rampersad, *Jackie Robinson*, p. 217.

18. "The Jackie Robinson Story," *Ebony*, June 1950, p. 92. Cited in Rampersad, *Jackie Robinson*, p. 225.

19. Rampersad, *Jackie Robinson*, p. 225.

20. *Sporting News*, July 12, 1950. Cited in Rampersad, *Jackie Robinson*, p. 229.

21. Stout and Johnson, *Jackie Robinson*, p. 127.

22. *Pittsburgh Courier*, June 17, 1950. Cited in Rampersad, *Jackie Robinson*, p. 228.

23. David Shiner, "Jackie Robinson and the Third Age of Modern Baseball," in *Jackie Robinson: Race, Sports, and the American Dream* (Armonk, NY: M.E. Sharpe, 1998), pp. 149–156.

24. Robinson, *I Never Had It Made*, p. 92.

25. Carl E. Prince, *Brooklyn's Dodgers* (New York: Oxford University Press, 1996), p. 49.

26. *Sporting News*, May 30, 1951. Cited in Rampersad, *Jackie Robinson*, p. 237.

27. Robinson, "A Kentucky Colonel Kept Me in Baseball," pp. 82–90.

28. Robinson, "A Kentucky Colonel Kept Me in Baseball," pp. 82–90.

29. Roger Kahn, *The Boys of Summer* (New York: Perennial Library, 1987), p. xi.

30. Kahn, *Boys of Summer*, p. xvii.

Chapter 7

THE BOYS OF SUMMER, 1952–1954

Robinson took what he intended to be one last barnstorming tour after the playoff series ended. The rigors of traveling through the segregated South for an entire month made these tours harder and harder for him to take. But the fan response was so loving—and the money was so good—that he decided to hit the road again. This year Campanella led his own team of all-stars. Robinson's squad included Larry Doby, Luke Easter of the Cleveland Indians, and Sam Jethroe of the Boston Braves. Five major-league teams had fielded black players in 1952, and almost every club now had black athletes under contract in their farm systems.

The rest of Robinson's off-season was filled with a busy schedule of charity events and speaking engagements, which he used to discuss the issue of racial equality as well as baseball. There were business deals, too. Most intriguing was the position he accepted at the New York City affiliate of the NBC television network. WNBC hired Robinson as its vice president and director of community activities, a job that promised on-air appearances as well as additional youth outreach work in the city. Robinson, looking toward a future outside of sports, saw the position as "a new turning point" in his career.[1] As far as baseball was concerned, the 1952 contract he signed in January guaranteed him a $42,000 salary.

The Dodgers gathered in Vero Beach for spring training with a renewed sense of purpose. The playoff loss to the Giants made them even more determined to take the pennant. It was a blow to learn that Don Newcombe had been drafted to serve in the military; the fastballer would not appear with the Dodgers in 1952 or 1953. The club added two young pitchers to fill his formidable shoes, Billy Loes and Joe Black.

Black, a college graduate, had pitched for the Baltimore Elite Giants before entering the Dodgers farm system. Like many young black athletes, he was in awe of Robinson, and meeting him made an indelible impression. "He says, 'Hey, you're big,'" Black recalled years later. "'You can fight too, can't you?' I said, 'I sure can.' He looked at me—and I'll always remember that look—and he says, 'But we're not gonna fight.'...He tells me that they're gonna be calling us names wherever we go, whatever we do." Black was surprised at this, he said; it was five years since Robinson had broken the color line, and stories about onfield racial taunting had disappeared from the press. No, Robinson said, the abuse had never fully stopped. But whatever was shouted, he told Black, they would not react with violence: "'That's what they want us to do. And we're going to ignore them.'"[2]

Indeed, while Robinson was and would remain one of the most verbal and intense competitors in baseball, he never did resort to violence or to fisticuffs to get his point across, either on or off the field. "Believe me, he had to have some tremendous restraint to bring that off," teammate Carl Erskine and many others have said.[3]

Robinson was involved in a number of onfield eruptions during the season as his reputation as a bench jockey *par excellence* solidified. In May an umpire accused Robinson of hurling ethnic slurs at him during a game, a charge that Robinson denied vehemently but that many in baseball seemed inclined to believe. In July, when Robinson exploded in anger at a bad call, he went so far as to kick his glove around the infield; this image, captured by a photographer and printed in newspapers nationwide, helped to set his image as a hothead into concrete. "I know it's wrong for me to lose my temper. It doesn't do me any good," he said apologetically after the glove incident. But "when an umpire makes an obvious mistake it seems I automatically blow up."[4]

Black for his part followed Robinson's advice about fighting, but as a pitcher, he had his own way of responding to racism on the field. One time when he was on the mound in Cincinnati, he could hear the Reds bench singing the folk song "Old Black Joe." Black, who possessed pinpoint control, proceeded to impassively shoot fastballs at the heads of seven successive batters before the umpires tossed him from the game. "Musta been some crooners in the lot," he observed. The music stopped.[5]

The Dodgers exploded out of the gate: in the first two weeks of the season, Roy Campanella, Carl Furillo, and third baseman Billy Cox were all hitting over .400, and Robinson's bat was booming at a heady .448 clip. The fireworks resulted in an 8–2 record over the first 10 games.

The Dodgers played the Giants in their home opener on April 18. Their rivalry was fiercer now than ever after the way the 1951 season had ended. In the sixth inning, down by a run, Brooklyn had two outs and two men on when pinch-hitter Bobby Morgan hit a long line drive to left-center that looked sure to score the runners. But Willie Mays, the Giants' brilliant young center fielder, intercepted the ball with a flying leap. He crashed into the grass and lay there, stunned by the impact. When he came to, Mays saw Robinson strolling away.

"Jackie was coming out here to see if I was all right?" Mays asked, impressed.

"Are you nuts?" responded his manager, Leo Durocher. "He only came out here to see if you still had the ball in your glove!"[6]

A month into the season, on May 14, the Robinsons welcomed a new baby boy, David, into the family. Though David was healthy and the delivery went well, Rachel had to remain in the hospital when she developed a kidney infection. Her illness rattled Robinson, who was deeply devoted to his wife. A few weeks later, when Robinson was in St. Louis for a Dodger road trip, he received a frightening phone call from home: Rachel needed to be rushed into surgery. She had found a lump in her breast that her doctors believed was cancerous. Robinson sped back to New York to be with her through the ordeal. Afterward they learned the lump had not been a tumor, and that Robinson had rushed home needlessly. "But he wasn't angry about that," Rachel remembered. "He just had a tremendous sense of relief."[7]

Rachel's health seemed to weigh on Robinson's mind, and his hitting suffered after the cancer scare, recovering only in late August. His All-Star appearance this year began with a bang as he hit a first-inning home run to put the National League on the scoreboard. They went on to win the rain-shortened game 3–2. Overall his batting average dropped 30 points from the previous season to .308—respectable, but not quite "Robinsonian." He did, however, hit a major milestone: on August 9, in Philadelphia's Shibe Park, Robinson smacked the 1,000th hit of his major-league career in a 6–0 Dodgers win.

Though the Giants nipped at their heels during the last month of the season, the Dodgers stayed true to their resolve and took the National League pennant by a comfortable 4.5 game margin.

Robinson's team headed into another "subway" World Series on October 1 to face, once again, the Yankees. With hurlers like Black, Billy Loes, and Carl Erskine, Brooklyn finally had the pitching to go toe-to-toe with their perpetual Series rivals. The Yankees, featuring Allie Reynolds' pitching and Mickey Mantle's slugging, were as tough as they ever had been.

Black got the ball for Game One and held the Yankee offense down to two runs. Robinson and Duke Snider took Yankee ace Allie Reynolds deep and Pee Wee Reese homered off Ray Scarborough in the 4–2 Brooklyn victory. The Yankees answered with a 7–1 effort the next day on the strength of Vic Raschi's three-hitter. Preacher Roe went the distance for Brooklyn in Game Three at Yankee Stadium, which the Dodgers won 5–3. The game included a Reese-Robinson double steal that put them both in scoring position; score they did on the next play, a passed ball by Yankee catcher Yogi Berra. In Game Four the Bombers again responded with a win, this time a 2–0, four-hit shutout pitched by Reynolds.

With the series tied at 2–2, the teams battled for 11 innings in Game 5. The Dodgers cobbled together a 6–5 victory with some old-school station-to-station run production and Duke Snider's home run. All they needed now was one more win, and the elusive World Series championship would be theirs. The last two games were scheduled for their home park, Ebbets Field.

They could not seal the deal. The Yankees won Game Six by a score of 3–2 that included the first World Series home run by young centerfielder Mickey Mantle. Black started Game Seven, his third start in seven days, and he labored. Mantle homered once more and hit a run-scoring double as Reynolds continued to confound the Dodgers. The 4–2 Brooklyn loss meant the championship crown remained in the Bronx. Sportswriters and fans began to complain that the Dodgers were "chokers," that the team froze in the clutch.

Black, who had 15 saves and a 15–4 record in the games he started, won the Rookie of the Year award, the fifth black player in the National League to do so. Robinson, who had opened that door, was beginning to feel his age. For the first time he began to seriously talk about retirement. So much progress had been made, but as far as he was concerned, there was much left to do.

Shortly after the World Series loss, Robinson publicly accused the Yankees of racism. On November 30 he appeared on a television show called *Youth Wants to Know*, in which an audience of teenagers posed unscripted questions to prominent guests. One girl asked whether Robinson believed that the Yankees, with their all-white roster, were discriminating against black athletes. Robinson's first response was a simple "Yes." The Yankee players were "fine sportsmen and wonderful gentlemen," he said, but the team's management was clearly prejudiced. "There isn't a single Negro on the team now and there are very few in the entire Yankee farm system," he pointed out.[8]

His observation made headlines nationwide and caused Yankees general manager George Weiss to assert that the team would be glad to add a black player to its lineup when it found one "who can play good enough ball to win a place" on the team.[9] It was a defense that echoed that of the Boston Red Sox almost a decade before, at the time of Robinson's fruitless tryout. "I could have ducked that question," Robinson said later, "but if I had ducked it I wouldn't have been able to live with myself."[10] It seems he felt that way about many of the issues he "popped off" about, both on the field and off it. No matter how much criticism was heaped upon him afterward, Robinson simply could not, in good conscience, remain silent when he had a strong opinion.

A few days later Robinson launched a new business venture, a men's clothing store in Harlem. The Jackie Robinson Store was located on busy 125th Street, the famous neighborhood's major thoroughfare. Robinson, a sharp dresser himself, was fascinated by Harlem and excited to be part of its business scene. Best of all, he had convinced his old friend Jack Gordon to move to New York and manage the shop. Gordon and his family lived with the Robinsons in St. Albans for a time, joining a household that over the past year had also hosted Rachel's brother Chuck and his family. Robinson was turning out to be more like his mother than he had ever expected.

STILL WAITING FOR "NEXT YEAR"

In the off-season Robinson came to a quick contract agreement with the Dodgers' new general manager Buzzie Bavasi. His salary of $42,000 meant he was still the highest-paid player on the club, with the possible exception of Reese.

When he arrived in Vero Beach for spring training, however, the 34-year-old Robinson was overweight and out of playing shape. That gave Dressen the opening he needed to make some changes. Dressen wanted to find a spot on the roster for Jim "Junior" Gilliam, a switch-hitting second baseman who had an outstanding 1952 season in Montreal. During spring training, it became clear that Dressen planned to move Robinson to third base, citing his decreased mobility as his reason for the move, and insert Gilliam into the now-vacant second base spot.

The trouble was the Dodgers already had a third baseman, Billy Cox. The veteran Cox wasn't the team's strongest hitter, but he was one of the league's best defensive third basemen, and now Dressen proposed to make him a jack-of-all-trades utility man. Cox was furious at the idea of losing the job he did well and had held for the better part of five seasons. The New York papers ran stories about how unhappy Cox and other white players were at the idea of him ceding his position to a black man. Several team members rushed to squelch that story. "You couldn't dream up a better relationship than that we have between the white and Negro members of our team," said Erskine.[11]

Another problem was that Robinson himself was not very comfortable at third base, a position that calls for long throws across the diamond and great agility. Dressen began to move him around—to first base, to second, back to third, even into the outfield. Toward the end of May, Robinson graciously said, "It doesn't make any difference to me where I play, so . . . I might as well be where I could do the team the most good."[12] The newly versatile Robinson played at five different positions during the season, keeping his powerful bat in the lineup and allowing Gilliam and Cox to play mainly at their natural positions.

The increased flexibility meant that the Brooklyn lineup could be effective from top to bottom, and the team led all of baseball in every major batting category. The 955 runs they scored as a team was among the highest of all time. They were in first place at the All-Star break and never looked back: they clinched the pennant on September 12 and finished the season 13 games over the second-place Milwaukee (formerly Boston) Braves. Brooklyn's at-home winning percentage, .772, was the best the National League had seen since 1902. Roy Campanella was a big part of the team's success; this was another MVP year for him as he led the league with 142 RBI and hit 41 homers besides. But Dodgers were all over the list when it came to the year's hitting honors: Furillo won the league batting title with a .344 average, Snider led the league in slugging and runs scored, and Rookie of the Year Gilliam's 17 triples were tops in the National League. Robinson had a strong year, too; with his .329 batting average and 95 RBI, he was as much a threat as ever. Meanwhile, the pitching staff remained consistently strong.

One game late in August stands as an example of the passion of the Brooklyn team and its fans. The Cardinals were in town and their manager, former Dodger Ed Stanky, took the lead in taunting Robinson, who was nursing a sore left knee. Whenever Robinson came to bat, Stanky did a limping-ape routine in the visitors' dugout, complete with grunts, hoots, and under-armpit scratching. Much of the display was visible to the fans in the close quarters of Ebbets Field.

Robinson returned to the bench, quickly hand-lettered a sign on a piece of cardboard, and displayed it to the crowd. It said "How to make up a line-up—by Eddie Stanky," to needle the manager for a batting-order mistake he perpetrated earlier in the season. The fans roared their appreciation. Then his teammates found an even better way to answer: They walloped the Cards for 12 runs that inning. Stanky found himself the target of a cascade of boos from his former home-town fans each time he trudged to the mound to remove a pitcher. "It was a Dodger moment; it was a Brooklyn moment," one historian has written. "This was the last time St. Louis would openly exercise its anti-black bias against the Dodgers."[13]

Going into the World Series, the Dodgers were in great shape. They hadn't slacked off after clinching the pennant, but Dressen had taken the opportunity to give his pitchers some rest. The Brooklyn squad was as confident as a team that had lost so many close pennant races and World Series could be. "If we don't win it this time, we'll never win it," Robinson said.[14]

They didn't win it. Instead, the Yankees took their fifth straight World Series championship, still the all-time record. The series was a six-game fireworks display in which the teams combined for 17 home runs.

Erskine, a 20-game winner that season, was shaky in Game One and allowed the Yankees to take an early lead. The Brooklyn hitters responded, but it wasn't enough, and New York won the game 9–5. The Yankees tied Game Two on a home run by Billy Martin that dropped just over the left field fence. Robinson, playing left, blamed himself for letting the ball go out. "I trailed it; I should have caught it," he said afterward.[15] A Mickey Mantle homer won the game for New York, 4–2.

The two teams relocated to Ebbets Field for the next three games, and the Dodgers made it a series by winning two of them. In Game Three, Erskine no-hit the Yankees through four innings, striking out 14 batters, and then Robinson smashed a double off the right-field screen, teased Yankee pitcher Vic Raschi into a balk, and scored a run on Cox's bunt. The Dodgers won the game 3–2 on a Campanella home run. Game Four saw the Dodger hitters back in their regular-season form as they scored seven runs for an easy 7–3 win. But in Game Five, the Yankees slugged their way to an 11–7 victory, sending the series back to the Bronx.

Game Six was a must-win for Brooklyn, and their ace Erskine would have to be the man on the mound. But the challenge of pitching three games in six days proved to be too much for him, and the Yankees jumped out to a three-run lead. In the top of the sixth inning, Robinson manufactured a run in his patented fashion, with a double, a steal, and a run home on a teammate's single. The Dodgers tied the game in the top of the ninth, but the Yankees had another half-inning to go. A walk and two singles later, it was all over: they won the game 4–3 and the World Series four games to two. The old Brooklyn vow, "Wait 'til next year," was sounding more and more like a cruel joke on the borough.

BARNSTORMING AND HOUSE HUNTING

Robinson had planned never to barnstorm again, but the chance to tour the South with a mixed-race team was too much of a challenge to pass up. The Jackie Robinson Negro-White All-Stars broke new ground by including white major leaguers in a predominantly black lineup and by playing in places that officially barred interracial competition. Gil Hodges, former Dodger Ralph Branca, and the Baltimore Orioles' Bobby Young joined Robinson on the squad. The tour drew large crowds in several cities, but in Birmingham, Alabama and Memphis, Tennessee, the white players did not take the field. Officials in both cities had made it clear that mixed-race competitions would not be tolerated. Robinson was widely criticized for caving in to Jim Crow in these instances. He said later that the white players had chosen to sit the games out, not wanting to cause trouble. But he also insisted that in Birmingham it was local civil rights activists, then locked in a battle to remove the Jim Crow restrictions, who had "asked me not to disobey the law—the disturbance I would stir up would hurt their cause."[16]

While he was away, the Dodgers franchise was thrown into turmoil by its manager. Dressen hoped to return to the ballclub in 1954, but he wanted more job security than the Dodgers' customary one-year contract offered. O'Malley would not budge from the idea of a one-year deal. Dressen, insulted, walked out of negotiations and out of the organization. Robinson, who had developed a close and mutually respectful relationship with his manager, was terribly upset by Dressen's departure.

Robinson's life outside of baseball was in for changes, too. For several months Rachel, no longer happy in St. Albans, had been house hunting. The Sugar Hill neighborhood where they lived was regarded as quite exclusive. Residents of the mixed-race community included musicians like Ella Fitzgerald and Count Basie and fellow athletes like Roy Campanella. But the Robinsons found urban living uncomfortable. They craved more privacy, and as the children grew, they wanted more outdoor space as well. The decision to move out of New York City "stemmed from my parents' belief that the country was the best place to raise children," daughter Sharon Robinson would say later.[17]

They went house hunting in the Westchester and Connecticut suburbs, but the Robinsons repeatedly received subtle and not-so-subtle signals from brokers and real estate agents that wherever they were looking was "not their place." For a long time Rachel had had the idea of a modern dream house in the back of her mind, and soon she decided that the best course would be to find a piece of land on which they could build it.

But that, too, proved troublesome. On at least one occasion she made a full-price offer on a property, only to be told that it had suddenly gone off the market.

But by now the Robinsons had no compunction about confronting discrimination head-on. When a reporter at a Connecticut newspaper got wind of the problem and contacted Rachel, she spoke openly about it.[18] The publicity spurred some equality-minded Connecticut residents to take action.

Andrea and Dick Simon were particularly upset. Dick, who ran the Simon and Schuster publishing house, and Andrea, his socially prominent wife, had a home in North Stamford, Connecticut. She hosted a gathering of local clergy members and real estate agents to discuss the problem of racism in their community and to ensure that the Robinsons would get the help they needed. Rachel was invited to attend. As soon as the meeting ended, Andrea, Rachel, and a local broker took a tour of some nearby homes and lots for sale. When Rachel saw the property at 103 Cascade Road in Stamford, she knew it was the place. "View, privacy, water" is what she had dreamed of, and this piece of land had it all, including its own pond and a view of the town reservoir.[19] Robinson saw it a few days later and immediately agreed. This was where they would build their house.

Getting the house built could have been another struggle, but their new Stamford friends were again helpful. The property owner, Ben Gunnar, was also a builder. He agreed to build the house to the Robinsons' specifications on the land that he sold them. A Russian immigrant who didn't want to make waves in his adopted home town, Gunnar initially feared community opposition to the deal. But his worries were soon eased by the owners of State National Bank in Stamford, who sympathized with the Robinsons and secured a mortgage for them quickly.[20]

One thing they had not anticipated, however, was the criticism that was aimed at them when word got out about their plans. "When it became known that we were building a big, modern house in a section of North Stamford where no other Negroes live, many people, colored and white alike, got worked up," Robinson wrote while the house was still under construction. "I guess most of them felt that I was moving into a place where I really didn't belong."[21] Black newspapers and columnists in particular accused him of trying to run away from his race, an especially hurtful charge.

Robinson spent much of the off season on a speaking tour for the National Conference of Christians and Jews, a group that promoted harmony among those of different races and faiths. It was a tentative step into the field that truly interested him: politics and advocacy, especially in the area of racial equality. In December the court case known as *Brown v. Board of Education* was argued before the Supreme Court. *Brown* challenged the entire Jim Crow structure by focusing on its "separate and unequal" effect on public education. In a few more months, the Court's unanimous decision that educational segregation was unconstitutional would effectively launch the Civil Rights Movement. With such changes in the air, Robinson resigned from his vice president's job at NBC. It was nothing but a figurehead position, he had found, and he wanted something more meaningful for his future.

CLUBHOUSE TROUBLE

Robinson soon became dissatisfied with his new manager, too. O'Malley had decided to promote Walter Alston, the Montreal Royals' skipper, into Dressen's old job. In the minors Alston had managed Campanella, Erskine, Black, Gilliam, Newcombe, and other current Dodgers, so he was familiar with many of the players. But he was a quiet, almost passive presence in the dugout, and he had practically no major-league experience in any capacity. Robinson, who had loved playing for Dressen, saw Alston as nothing more than O'Malley's lackey, and Alston knew it. Their relationship would remain cool at best for the rest of Robinson's career.

Robinson batted over .350 in the first three months of the season but bounced between left field and third base as Alston tried to get playing time for young outfielder Sandy Amoros. On April 23 in a game against Pittsburgh, he proved that he still had enough of his old speed and smarts to put together a dazzling base-running play when he stole home as the lead runner in a confounding triple steal. Then in the thirteenth inning, Robinson won the game with a double that brought Junior Gilliam home.

The Dodger veterans, who were increasingly feeling their age, intended to repeat their pennant win and get one more shot at the world championship. The Giants were not about to make it easy for them, though. The New York team had regained the phenomenal Willie Mays from his stint in the Army and had added a talented young pitcher, Johnny Antonelli. In May the Giants put together a dizzying 24–4 run, and when the two teams met for a three-game series in late June, the Giants swept it. The whole Brooklyn squad was frustrated, none more than the ultra-competitive Robinson, who had more serious onfield blowups in this season than ever before.

On June 2 in Milwaukee, Robinson was steaming because of a bad call by the home-plate umpire, Lee Ballanfant. The Braves' Johnny Logan was at the plate with a 2–2 count. When a scoreboard screwup accidentally displayed the count as 3–2, Ballanfant became confused. He called the next pitch a ball and gave Logan a walk, loading the bases. The Dodgers exploded in protest, and Robinson ran all the way in from left field to participate in their 15-minute argument, but the call stood. The next batter, Eddie Mathews, smashed a grand slam.

When Robinson came to bat in the fifth inning, he asked Ballanfant, "Can I get a walk on three balls the way Logan did?" Ballanfant took offense at that, and after further words were exchanged, he threw Robinson out of the game. As the ballplayer stalked away, "I flipped the bat toward the dugout," he wrote a few months later. "It was a wet night, and the bat slipped. It landed on the roof of the dugout, bounced into the stands and hit three spectators. So my reputation as a sorehead and a poor sport was clinched."[22] The rest of the team, still furious, scored five runs in the rest of the inning and won the game.

Later in the season, the Dodgers were in Wrigley Field to play the Chicago Cubs when Duke Snider hit a home run. At least it looked like a home run to Robinson, sitting in the visitors' dugout. "I saw it clear the wall," he said. "Then it struck a spectator and dropped onto the playing field... We saw the spectator double up, clutching at his stomach in pained surprise."[23]

The umpire didn't see it that way. He assumed the ball had bounced off the left-field wall and called it a ground-rule double.

Robinson shot out of the dugout and headed straight to the ump to challenge the ruling. The whole bench had seen what he had seen, he was sure. But no other Dodger, not even manager Alston, came out with him. When he realized he was alone in his protest, Robinson said, "I felt foolish. I wanted to find a hole and crawl into it...I knew I had no right to be out there arguing a play in which I hadn't figured at all. But my team had. It kills me to lose, and when I ran out to question [the] decision, I never took a second to think."[24]

The next day's papers ran photos that proved Robinson had been right all along, but it didn't much matter. The image of him as an argumentative hothead only broadened and deepened in the wake of incidents like these.

Life on the road for the Dodgers' black players had improved somewhat over the years but was still problematic. St. Louis remained one of the most stubbornly segregated towns on the circuit. Most of the team was able to stay at the comfortably air-conditioned Chase Hotel, but the black players were relegated to the Adams, an old-fashioned place that was unbearable in the steamy summer heat. In 1954 the Chase finally relented—a bit.

The hotel management told the Dodgers that their black players might stay there, as long as they did not use such public facilities as the dining room, nightclub, or pool.

Offended at the restrictions, most of the black players chose to go back to the Adams. "But Jackie said he was staying," Joe Black remembered. "Jackie says, 'I'm not gonna let them chase me out of here, that's what they want. I'm staying right here.'"[25] Robinson stayed at the hotel and in the management's face for the rest of his baseball career, challenging their boundaries all that time. Gradually, the restrictions eased and then disappeared.

The incident at the Chase was one that threw a spotlight on the relationship between Robinson and Roy Campanella. To Campanella, refusing the hotel's limited offer and loyally sticking with the Adams was a matter of pride. To Robinson, accepting the Chase's conditions while fighting to change them was worth whatever trouble it might cause. "I'm no crusader," Campanella maintained.[26]

Indeed he was not. Campanella was on off-field favorite among the predominantly white reporters who covered the team. The writers found Robinson prickly but quotable; they found Campanella genial and friendly. In reality, Campanella was just as fierce a competitor as Robinson, but he saw his role on the team as a very different one. "It was my position, catching," he explained later. "A catcher has to make people like him, no matter what," because he needs to be able to call pitches, direct the positioning of the fielders, and act as the team's onfield general. Many analysts assumed that Campanella's easygoing attitude was a result of his Philadelphia upbringing, of his mixed-race heritage, or of a naturally cheerful personality. Campanella insisted it was none of these things. As a catcher, he said, "I had to make everyone on the team work with me. I had to have a sunny disposition. I had to keep the tempo up. You can't be demanding. You got to have a piece of sugar in your hand." Campanella saw himself as a catcher first and a black man second, and during his playing days that attitude set him and Robinson apart.[27]

Back at home, the Robinson family set themselves apart when they moved out of New York City and into the leafy suburbs of Fairfield County, Connecticut. Their house was still under construction as builder Ben Gunnar labored to get every detail exactly right. To give Jackie Junior a chance to start school locally, and to help Rachel be close enough to monitor the building site, Andrea Simon offered the Robinsons temporary use of her family's large Connecticut home. After all, the Simons had residences in New York City and Martha's Vineyard as well. The Robinsons hesitated to accept this generous suggestion, but the logic of it was undeniable, and

Rachel and Andrea had developed a strong friendship. In late August she and the children moved into the Simons' lovely colonial home, set on 50 acres of land that included its own apple orchard, and began to settle into the country life she had dreamed of.

At the end of the season, the Dodgers took second place in the pennant race, five games behind the Giants. Though Robinson suffered a terrible slump in July, his strong start ensured him a respectable .311 average. He played mainly in left field once again, and he started 50 games at third as well. But his speed had clearly declined; Robinson stole only seven bases all year. Campanella, too, had a difficult season, as a hand injury restricted his motion. He went from 41 home runs in 1953 to only 19 in 1954, and from 142 to 51 runs batted in. Still, Brooklyn had managed to score a league-leading 778 runs, largely off the bats of Duke Snider, Gil Hodges, and Junior Gilliam.

Losing the pennant to their cross-town rival was bad enough. Watching the Giants head to the World Series and actually win it in a four-game sweep of the Cleveland Indians—that really hurt. "Next year" never seemed as far away as it did in the fall of 1954.

NOTES

1. Arnold Rampersad, *Jackie Robinson: A Biography* (New York: Ballantine Books, 1998), p. 243.

2. David Falkner, *Great Time Coming: The Life of Jackie Robinson from Baseball to Birmingham* (New York: Simon and Schuster, 1995), p. 219.

3. Falkner, *Great Time Coming*, p. 218.

4. *Pittsburgh Courier*, July 26, 1952. Cited in Rampersad, *Jackie Robinson*, p. 246.

5. Roger Kahn, *The Boys of Summer* (New York: Perennial Library, 1987), p. 153.

6. Willie Mays and Lou Sahadi, *Say Hey: The Autobiography of Willie Mays* (New York: Simon and Schuster, 1988), p. 82.

7. Rampersad, *Jackie Robinson*, pp. 247–248.

8. *Pittsburgh Courier*, December 27, 1952. Cited in Rampersad, *Jackie Robinson*, p. 253.

9. *Pittsburgh Courier*, December 27, 1952. Cited in Rampersad, *Jackie Robinson*, p. 253.

10. Jackie Robinson, "Your Temper Can Ruin Us!" *Look*, February 22, 1955, pp. 78–87.

11. *Pittsburgh Courier*, March 28, 1953. Cited in Rampersad, *Jackie Robinson*, p. 257.

12. *Pittsburgh Courier*, June 6, 1953. Cited in Rampersad, *Jackie Robinson*, p. 257.

13. Carl E. Prince, *Brooklyn's Dodgers: The Bums, the Borough, and the Best of Baseball* (New York: Oxford University Press, 1996), p. 15.

14. *Pittsburgh Courier*, September 26, 1953. Cited in Rampersad, *Jackie Robinson*, p. 259.

15. Glen Stout and Dick Johnson, *Jackie Robinson: Between the Baselines* (San Francisco: Woodford Press, 1997), p. 147.

16. Robinson, "Your Temper Can Ruin Us!" pp. 78–87.

17. Sharon Robinson, *Stealing Home* (New York: HarperPerennial, 1997), p. 23.

18. Rampersad, *Jackie Robinson*, p. 273.

19. Kahn, *The Boys of Summer*, p. 405.

20. Rampersad, *Jackie Robinson*, p. 274.

21. Robinson, Jackie. "Now I Know Why They Boo Me!" *Look*, January 15, 1955, pp. 22–28.

22. Robinson, "Now I Know Why They Boo Me!" pp. 22–28.

23. Robinson, "Now I Know Why They Boo Me!" pp. 22–28.

24. Robinson, "Now I Know Why They Boo Me!" pp. 22–28.

25. Falkner, *Great Time Coming*, p. 235. Black recalled that the incident occurred during the 1953 season, but other sources pinpoint the date of Robinson's first registration at the Chase as April 27, 1954.

26. Jackie Robinson, *I Never Had It Made* (New York: Ecco, 1995), p. 96.

27. Jackie Robinson, *Baseball Has Done It* (Brooklyn, NY: Ig Publishing, 2005), pp. 92–93.

Chapter 8

TRIUMPH AND DECLINE, 1955–1956

After the 1954 season, Robinson felt battered physically and emotionally. His career as an athlete was coming to an end. Through an attorney friend he began making contacts in the business world in hopes of lining up a meaningful, interesting job outside of baseball. He didn't want to be a figurehead or a token as he had been at the television station.

In February of 1955 the Robinson family finally moved into their brand-new house in Stamford. It was set on six private acres that overlooked the town reservoir (a sweet reward for a man who had been chased out of his hometown reservoir as a child). There were woods on three sides, maximizing privacy. The house was built with children in mind. Jackie, now age six; Sharon, four; and David, two, each had his or her own room, complete with guest bed to allow for friends to stay overnight. The basement level contained recreation rooms, and the house included such delights as "secret" stairways, a fireman's pole to slide on, and private nooks. And they loved having all that land to explore.[1]

At the same time, the home's details and finishings had been chosen according to Rachel's taste. Her daughter Sharon described its towering stone fireplaces and paneling of African mahogany, and most impressive of all, a bathtub "the size of a small swimming pool [with] brass faucets curved in the shape of arched fish."[2]

All this loveliness came with a steep price tag, however. The Robinsons paid more than $90,000 for the house, an extravagant amount at the time.

Partly so as to keep up with the mortgage payments, Robinson joked, he signed his 1955 contract for a reported $40,000 and arrived at spring training as usual. Billy Cox had been traded, and Robinson set his sights on third base. He faced serious competition for the slot from much younger players, especially Don Hoak, who had played half of the previous season at third, and Don Zimmer. Robinson worked harder than ever to get his 36-year-old body in shape, but all the exercise seemed to do was give him a sore arm.

During the 1954 season, Robinson's relationship with manager Walter Alston had worsened. Alston was not a demonstrative presence on the field, and as Robinson went through the season arguing calls and jawing at umpires, Alston stood impassively by. The player soon resented his manager's lack of support and began to suspect a racial undercurrent. By September the two men did not seem to be able to talk together at all, and they increasingly sent their messages to one another through the press.

Robinson hoped to undo the damage in spring training, and at first both men seemed to want a fresh start. But within a few weeks they were at it again: Alston was quoted in the *Herald Tribune* saying that Hoak might win the third baseman's job outright; Robinson responded in the *Daily News*, calling himself a Dodger "irregular" and demanding to be traded if Alston didn't plan to play him every day. The two nearly came to blows in a preseason clubhouse meeting Alston called to complain about players who took their gripes to the press. It was a poisonous way to start the season.

Strangely, though, the strain didn't seem to hurt the team a bit. The core of the Dodgers—Campanella, Hodges, Reese, Snider, Furillo, and Robinson—remained stable, as it had since the opening day of 1949. These players owed their loyalties to one another and to the team, not to their manager. It may be, as some writers have speculated, that their shared dislike of Alston propelled them to the heights of the 1955 season. They did not know it in April, but for Brooklyn "next year" had finally arrived.

NO MORE WAITING

The Dodgers roared out of the gate with a ten-game winning streak that set a National League record. Robinson, who started the Opening Day game at third base after all, celebrated with a cunning break-up of a double play. Robinson was at second base when Campanella sent a soft groundball toward the Pirates' shortstop. It would have been an easy pair of outs but for Robinson. Heads-up as always, he let the batted ball hit him as he went from second to third. According to the rules, that meant

Robinson was out but the batter, Campanella, was safe and was credited with a hit. The Dodgers won the game 6–1.

The team looked strong from the get-go and only improved as it went. Pitcher Don Newcombe, back from his Army hitch, went 18–1 through July. Snider, Gilliam, and Campanella led the offense. The pennant seemed a sure bet early on; after their initial streak, Brooklyn put together a 22–3 record over the first four weeks of the season.

Their early run was marred only by the viciousness of the team's first home series with the world champion Giants. The rivalry between the two clubs had always been fierce, and particularly so since Leo Durocher went from managing one to the other. Robinson claimed that he and Durocher had been "friendly" ever since he went to the Giants clubhouse to congratulate them after the Miracle of Coogan's Bluff in 1951, but all those warm feelings disappeared whenever they took the field. The two continued to viciously bait one another during games. "I could not repeat the things we said to one another," Robinson had written modestly in a magazine piece that winter.[3]

The Dodgers-Giants matchups of 1955 were nastier than ever. It was the Giants who broke Brooklyn's winning streak at Ebbets Field on April 22. The next day Sal Maglie came to the mound for New York. Maglie was the master of the brushback pitch, a ball that comes into the batter high and tight to move him back off the plate. He would follow it with a low and outside curveball that was impossible to reach. Egged on, no doubt, by Durocher, he regarded Robinson as a special target (although, to be fair, Maglie threw at everybody), and the two had a long and contentious history.

In this game, Maglie "shaved" Dodger after Dodger with close pitches right under their chins and came especially close to beaning Campanella and Robinson. By the bottom of the fourth inning, with the score tied 1–1, the Dodgers decided that something had to be done about him. Robinson would drop a bunt up the first-base line. Giants first baseman Whitey Lockman would come off the bag to field it. Maglie would cover first. And Robinson would flatten him with all the force the former halfback could muster.

It all went as planned—the bunt was perfect, Lockman fielded it, and Robinson steamrolled the Giant covering first. Except that the Giant at first base was not Maglie. The pitcher, seeing the play develop, hung back. His slight 160-pound second baseman, Davey Williams, dashed to the bag instead. Robinson practically ran through him, shouldering Williams in the midsection and flinging him into the air. Williams was badly hurt; he played off and on for the rest of the season, but the injury essentially ended his baseball career.

The Giants were incensed and made a plan of their own: the next man who got anywhere near third base would take Robinson out the same way. In the fifth inning Giants captain Alvin Dark hit a double and kept going. A former college football star himself, Dark barreled straight toward Robinson. Robinson, who got the throw from the outfield in plenty of time, stepped nimbly aside and tagged Dark hard in the face. His one regret was that the ball popped free in the process, leaving Dark safe.

After the game, which Brooklyn won 3–1, Robinson insisted his run into Williams was an accident (later he clarified that in the heat of the moment he did not see that it was Williams and not Maglie at the bag), but his teammates openly thanked him for protecting them. Dark asked the newsmen to tell Robinson that they were even now and proceeded to call him "a Hitler" in private.

While the Dodgers continued to win, Robinson saw less playing time than ever. He had become convinced that his club's owner and manager were borderline racists who had it in for him because he "was not O'Malley's kind of Negro"—cheerful, easygoing, and meek. And he was becoming more and more agitated about the civil rights cause, as some in the South and elsewhere reacted violently against the Supreme Court's 1954 *Brown* ruling and its obvious implications for segregation. Church burnings, lynchings, and other crimes meant to frighten blacks into submission were on the rise, and Robinson followed these developments with mounting alarm.

When Pee Wee Reese was honored with a well-deserved fan appreciation night in July, the grounds crew raised eight Confederate flags over Ebbets Field to salute the shortstop's Southern heritage. Robinson was livid. However highly he thought of Reese, to Robinson "it was as if Jim Crow had opened up the gate to center field and trotted in to play, mitt in hand," Carl Erskine wrote later. "Jackie saw the Confederate flags as representing an evil empire—an empire against human dignity and racial equality." After the game he raged through the clubhouse, furious. His teammates tried to explain that the grounds crew meant the flag-raising to be nothing but an affectionate gesture, and they couldn't understand why Robinson was, as Erskine put it, "as hot as I'd seen him...he felt this was an indignity done to him in his own house."[4] A full decade after he'd joined the Dodgers organization, Robinson could still be a cipher to his teammates.

Robinson missed a number of games in the middle part of the season, sidelined by his increasingly creaky knee and ankle, but as the Dodgers went into the stretch, his innate competitiveness drove him back into the lineup. He made a conscious decision to "go out there and hustle," he told reporters. "I felt if I started running, the others might take the cue. You know something? It worked."[5] In a game against the Cubs in Chicago, for example, Robinson's taunts—"You can't get me out, you big slob!"—made pitcher Sam Jones so flustered that he threw every ball out of the strike zone, giving Robinson a walk.[6] Robinson proceeded to inform the hapless Jones that he would now steal second, then third, then home, all of which he did. There would be no late-season collapse for the 1955 Dodgers if Robinson had anything to say about it.

It was no surprise when the Dodgers won the league title by 13.5 games over Milwaukee. They clinched the pennant on September 8 while on the road. It was the earliest the National League championship had ever been decided. When they returned to Brooklyn on September 16, the team was greeted by a huge crowd of 300,000 fans who lined Flatbush Avenue and Fulton Street to welcome them home.

Two days later, in a departure from Dodger tradition, Walter O'Malley confirmed that Alston would be the club's manager again in 1956. Perhaps bolstered by this vote of confidence, Alston was proactive enough to call several pre-series team meetings to fire up his troops as they prepared to face the Yankees once again.

Robinson had played only 105 games during the regular season, the fewest of his career. His batting average fell to .256, a sharp drop-off after six straight seasons of hitting .300 or better, and he had only 36 RBI and 12 stolen bases. He was 36 years old and beginning to feel like it. None of that mattered to him. The World Series was on the line, and he knew full well that this might be his last chance.

Despite his loss of speed, Robinson was still a terror on the basepaths, never more so than in Game One of the World Series. Don Newcombe, who had won 20 games for Brooklyn but had faltered in the second half, was touched by Yankee batters for three homers that scored five of their six runs. The Dodgers in turn chipped away at Yankee ace Whitey Ford with a Robinson triple and home runs by Furillo and Snider. The score was 6–3, with one man on and one out, when Robinson came to the plate in the eighth inning. He smashed the ball toward left and the Yankee third baseman misplayed it, putting Furillo on third and Robinson on second. Zimmer hit a long sacrifice fly that scored Furillo and moved Robinson to third base.

With two outs and the team at bat down by two in a game's late innings, it is against all baseball wisdom for a man on third to break for home. The risk is too great, and even a successful steal would not be enough to win. It is simply not done. Secure in this knowledge, Yankee lefthander Whitey Ford faced first base and went into his windup.

Robinson broke for home.

With a good lead and his outstanding acceleration, he was bearing down on home base in a heartbeat. Yankee catcher Yogi Berra saw him coming and jumped forward over the plate to receive the pitch that Ford had by now released. Robinson went into a slide, right leg extended, toe pointing too. Berra caught the ball and swept his mitt down to make the tag.

Whether he did or didn't tag Robinson in time remains a matter of debate decades later. Umpire Bill Summers immediately called Robinson safe. Berra, apoplectic, was arguing the call even as he was rising out of his crouch. He insists to this day that he got the tag down. After the game Robinson snorted, "The only ridiculous thing about that play was the Yankees' squawking about me being called safe. There wasn't any question about it. I was over the plate before Berra got the ball on me."[7]

Much later, Robinson conceded that the steal attempt "was not the best baseball strategy," but that his real goal had been to wake his team up.[8] His mad dash made the score 6–5, and there it remained. For all Robinson's daring, Brooklyn lost the game.

They lost Game Two the next day, 4–2, and the press corps pounced. This was Brooklyn's seventh attempt at the World Series crown, the papers reminded a rapt city. They had lost all six previous tries. Were they about to blow another chance? After all, not since 1921 had a team come back to win the series after losing the first two games, and that was in a best-five-of-nine format. Robinson did his part in Game Two, scoring the team's second run in the fifth inning, but that was all from the National League champions. "If ever the Dodgers are to win a world series," lectured one reporter, "somebody will have to take them in hand and give them some fresh ideas."[9]

The new idea for Game Three turned out to be pitcher Johnny Podres, who had had a middling 9–10 season but now became Brooklyn's postseason hero. He threw a complete game for an 8–3 Dodgers win at Ebbets Field.

They tied the series up by winning Game Four 8–5. This was a day for the sluggers as Campanella, Hodges, and Snider all connected for home runs. Then, against the odds, Brooklyn won their third game in a row. In Game Five their rookie pitcher Roger Craig, who had joined the team in midseason, held the Yankees to one run over six innings and reliever Clem Labine gave up two, while Duke Snider hit two home runs and a double. Robinson added another run with an eighth-inning single to help Brooklyn win Game Five by a 5–3 score.

When the series returned to the Bronx, the spell was broken. Brooklyn's Karl Spooner seemed to have no control of his fastball, and he gave up five quick runs in the first inning. The Dodgers could not recover; they lost the game 5–1.

It all came down to Game Seven on the afternoon of October 4 at Yankee Stadium, and all of New York followed the game pitch by pitch on the radio or on television. So many people were tuned in to the game that, as one resident remembered, "you could walk for 10 blocks through Brooklyn, and never miss an at-bat" as the sounds of the game poured out through open windows and piped from transistor radios on every stoop.[10]

Alston decided to give the ball to Podres, the hero of Game Three, rather than the clearly exhausted Don Newcombe. Robinson, too, remained on the bench; he had injured his heel during one of his base-running escapades. Podres responded with a complete-game gem, allowing eight hits but no rallies and shutting the Yankees out. Gil Hodges was responsible for all of the Brooklyn scoring—he batted Campanella home with a double in the fourth inning, then hit a sacrifice fly that garnered him another RBI in the sixth. Sandy Amoros's heroic running catch of a hard-hit Berra fly ball in the bottom of that inning, which he whipped back to the infield for a surprise double play, preserved the shutout. The Dodgers won the game 2–0 for the franchise's first-ever World Series championship, and Brooklyn exploded with elation. From cheering in the streets to singing in the subways to yelling out of windows, fans throughout the borough and beyond celebrated with their team.

For once, Robinson didn't even mind being on the bench. Being on a World Series champion team was thrill enough.[11]

THE END OF AN ERA

That month marked the tenth anniversary of Robinson's recruitment by the Dodgers, now universally recognized as a major milestone in American history. Newspapers and magazines commemorated the event, and the November issue of *Ebony* went so far as to dub the previous decade "the Jackie Robinson Era." Robinson was still an active player, but it was clear that his career was very near its end. The stress of those early years of the "Great Experiment" had taken a visible toll. Already articles about his life in baseball were threaded with an elegiac tone: "It is largely because of Jackie—the way he played, the gull he took, the spirit he showed—that Negro players today can enter baseball, and other sports, like men, not beggars for a chance."[12] Meanwhile, the still-vigorous Campanella won the National League's most valuable player award for the third time.

Several weeks later, on December 1, Rosa Parks struck her famous blow against racism and segregation by refusing to move to the back of a Montgomery, Alabama bus. Robinson was struck by the parallel between Parks' act of defiance and his own Army court-martial. Over the next few months the anti-segregation resistance movement grew rapidly, led by the young black Montgomery ministers Ralph David Abernathy and Martin Luther King, Jr. Their cause "had great impact on us," Rachel would say later. "We were inspired by the courage and tenacity of these Southerners."[13] Robinson continued to speak for the National Conference of Christians and Jews during this off-season, but he also began to take a deeper interest in the workings of the NAACP and in Dr. King's efforts.

Near the end of January, Robinson signed what would be his final contract with the Brooklyn Dodgers. The agreement cut Robinson's pay to $33,000, and reporters writing about the deal had no compunction about referring to him as a "fading athlete."[14]

As insurance, the Dodgers traded Don Hoak to Chicago for another third baseman, Randy Jackson. Robinson knew that his legs could not handle too many games in the outfield, and he set his sights once again on the job at third. He worked hard at his conditioning and started the season there, batting sixth. Jackson remained on the roster as a backup third sacker.

The ballclub had a more intractable problem than Robinson to deal with, however. For years now Walter O'Malley had tried to build a new stadium for the Dodgers. Ebbets Field, for all its atmosphere, was falling apart. But New York City politics had blocked his plans at every turn. Now O'Malley was threatening to remove the team from Brooklyn altogether. The Boston Braves had successfully relocated to Milwaukee, after all; why stay in New York if he could get so little cooperation? The Dodgers owner floated rumors of moves to Minnesota, to California, even to Mexico City.

To show Brooklyn he meant business, O'Malley arranged for the Dodgers to play seven of their 1956 home games in New Jersey—in Jersey City's Roosevelt Stadium, in fact, the site of Robinson's triumphant entry into minor-league baseball. On April 19, almost 10 years to the day from that brilliant contest, Robinson and the Dodgers met the St. Louis Cardinals there for the second game of the baseball season.

If Robinson had imagined a warm welcome from a nostalgic crowd, he was very much mistaken. The Jersey City fans were out for blood. They booed and catcalled every move the Dodgers and Robinson made. Locals were asked why this was so, and they gave a plethora of reasons: the ballpark's previous tenant had been a New York Giants affiliate, making everyone in Jersey City a die-hard Giants fan; the people saw they were only pawns in O'Malley's stadium game, and they resented it; they just plain liked to boo. ("They'll boo anyone or anything," one longtime resident said.) Robinson, however, saw it his own way. After another Jersey City game, he stormed through the clubhouse shouting "Racists, racists, racists!"[15]

Whatever the reason it was a shocking start for the new World Champions. And Robinson wasn't the only Dodger who was feeling old. The veteran-heavy club got off to a sluggish start and remained back in the standings for the first two months of the season as Cincinnati, Milwaukee, Pittsburgh, and St. Louis battled for the upper berths. Robinson tried hard to live up to his own standards: on April 25 he stole home for what would be the last time in his career, in a game against the Giants at the Polo Grounds.

If that was meant as a slap at his cross-town rivals, it was returned on May 15 when the Dodgers bought the contract of former Giant Sal Maglie, the man at the center of so many past beanball wars and Robinson's particular enemy. Robinson, however, was the first to welcome Maglie to the clubhouse. For as far back as 1948, he had been the team's unofficial greeter, bringing new players into what they all regarded as the "Dodger family." Besides, now that Maglie was on his side, he wouldn't be aiming at Robinson's head anymore. Now 39 and nearing the end of his own career, Maglie responded, going 13–5 for his new team with a 2.89 earned run average and 110 strikeouts.

Toward the middle of the season, as Brooklyn improved and moved up in the standings, Robinson slumped. He may have been feeling the early symptoms of an as-yet undiagnosed case of diabetes, though at the time most assumed that his loss of coordination and speed were simply due to age. The effect was the same: Jackson was playing third while Robinson sat on the bench. He worried that his skills would become less and less sharp the longer he "rode the pine," but he kept his spirits up and his head in the game with a constant stream of chatter: encouragement and advice for his fellow Dodgers, insults and catcalls for their opponents. "I like Jack's attitude," Alston had to admit. "I like the way he peps up the bench."[16]

By the end of July, Alston was using him in important games again, and his trust paid off in a contest with the Braves in Jersey City. Robinson hit a two-run home run to put the Dodgers ahead, keyed a clutch double play in the ninth inning with the score tied and the bases loaded, and won the game with a well-placed fly ball to deep center field. He could still turn it on when it counted.

That ability was even more important in September. The Braves held a two-game edge over the rest of the league, but Brooklyn surged just as

Milwaukee faltered. Robinson played like a man possessed in this final month. Not only did his hitting improve markedly, his base-running created opportunities that his team was quick to exploit. In a crucial game against the Braves, he faked a step toward third from his perch on second base. The Braves pitcher attempted a pickoff and botched the throw, sending the ball into center field and Robinson all the way home. Rattled, the pitcher surrendered a home run to Hodges, the next Dodger batter, and that was the ballgame.

A few days later, Maglie no-hit the Phillies, and Robinson tricked another pitcher into an errant pickoff throw. This one put two men in scoring position and set the stage for the Dodgers' first three runs of the game. They went on to win it 5–0.

On September 29, the final day of the season, Brooklyn took the pennant for the second year in a row, beating out the Braves by a single game. In the end it was their pitching that led the way as Don Newcombe and Johnny Antonelli combined for 47 wins (20 for Antonelli and a tremendous 27 for Newcombe, one of the best season totals of the modern era). Brooklyn pitchers threw two no-hitters during the season, Erskine against the Giants on May 12 and Maglie over Philadelphia on September 25. Who but the Yankees could be their postseason opponent?

The World Series started with Brooklyn taking the first two games at Ebbets Field. In Game One, Maglie gave up a two-run homer to Mickey Mantle early on, but the Brooklyn hitters answered in the second inning when Robinson hit a lead-off home run and Furillo doubled to score Hodges from first. They chased the Yankees' Whitey Ford off the mound with Hodges' three-run home run in the third and went on to win the game 6–3. Game Two set a record as the longest-ever nine-inning World Series contest as the Yankees burned through seven pitchers (another series record) in a 13–8 Brooklyn win.

When the series moved to Yankee Stadium, New York tied things up with wins in Games Three and Four. Robinson manufactured Brooklyn's first run in the second inning of Game Three in his classic station-to-station style, drawing a walk and moving around the diamond on singles and sacrifices. But the Yankees answered in their own fashion, with a three-run home run off the bat of Enos Slaughter, and won the game 5–3. Tom Sturdivant came close to shutting the Dodgers down in Game Four, allowing only two runs, one a ninth-inning double to Robinson that scored a run. By that point the Yankees were already up by five runs, three of which came from homers by Mantle and Hank Bauer, and the Bronx took the game 6–2.

Game Five was Don Larsen's triumphant perfect game in the Bronx. The Dodgers, who had notched two no-hitters during the course of the season, got a bitter taste of their own medicine. Maglie went the distance and kept things close, allowing only two runs. But none of the Dodgers could do anything against Larsen, and the Yankees went up 3–2 in the series.

Back in Brooklyn for Game Six, the two teams battled through nine scoreless innings, with Bob Turley on the mound for the Yankees and Clem Labine for the Dodgers. It was Robinson who broke the 0–0 tie after Turley walked Gilliam in the bottom of the tenth and intentionally walked Snider to pitch to the aging third baseman. Robinson fought back with a sharply hit, but catchable, fly to left field that sailed just over Slaughter's head. It caromed off the base of the wall and Slaughter missed it again. Gilliam scored, the Dodgers won 1–0, and the series was knotted again.

But that was the last run the Dodgers would score. In Game Seven, Yankee pitcher Johnny Kucks allowed only three hits in a 9–0 Bronx romp that gained the Bombers yet another World Series victory. Robinson was the man at bat with two out in the bottom of the ninth. With his team down by nine runs, there was nothing he could reasonably do to change the outcome. But Robinson treated every at-bat as if it mattered, and this one was no exception. He struck out, but in the excitement Yogi Berra dropped the ball, and Robinson dashed for first. Moose Skowron tagged him out there, and the game was over.

It was a disappointing season for Robinson, in spite of his clutch play down the stretch. He batted .275, stole 12 bases, and hit 10 home runs. All these matched or bettered his dismal 1955 numbers, but not by much. Robinson knew that his Game Six RBI would be his last.

TRAVELS AND TRADES

The Dodgers barely had time to catch a breath once the series was over before they were traveling again, this time to Japan for a six-week goodwill tour. Robinson joined the group, mainly because the Dodger wives had been invited along, and Rachel greatly wanted to go. They both enjoyed it immensely. With the children home in Connecticut under the care of Zellee Isum, they were free to sightsee, visit museums, and try local foods. Rachel noticed how relaxed her husband seemed. "I think he saw the tour of Japan as the culmination of his Dodger career," she said later. "He tried new things eagerly, which was not always the case at home. There he was, dressing up in kimonos, trying gamely to eat all kinds of unfamiliar food."[17] It was as if, with the end of his days as a Dodger in sight, he was trying to squeeze every last drop of enjoyment from them.

Shortly after his return home, Robinson was honored with an award that would help to shape the next few years of his life. It was the Springarn Medal, which was given each year by the NAACP for distinguished service to black people in the United States. Robinson was the first athlete to receive the medal in its 41-year history, and with it he joined rarefied company: scientist George Washington Carver, educator Mary McLeod Bethune, labor leader A. Philip Randolph, and poet James Weldon Johnson were all Springarn recipients. To Robinson, Rachel said, the medal meant "that his accomplishments on the field had significance beyond sports—and that he himself was needed in the ranks of black leadership."[18] In the next year Robinson would begin to take on more and more tasks for the organization.

Around that same time, Robinson was contacted by William H. Black, founder and president of the Chock full o'Nuts coffee company. The two men met and developed a quick rapport. A few days later Black offered Robinson the kind of substantial job he had been looking for: vice president and director of personnel in his company. Robinson jumped at the chance. He was tired of the road trips, tired of the arguments, tired of the injuries, tired of reporters—just tired. His work in baseball was done; his family needed him at home. Still, Jackie Junior and David burst into tears when he told them the news. Sharon, who loved the idea of having her father home more, was overjoyed.

Outside the family, however, his decision to leave baseball had to be kept secret for the moment. Two years before, Robinson had sold exclusive rights to his retirement story to *Look* magazine for $50,000. The issue carrying the news would hit the stands on January 8, 1957.

Unknowingly, the Dodgers inserted themselves into this civilized arrangement and turned it all upside-down. On the very day Robinson was scheduled to give his story to the *Look* editors and sign his contract with Black, general manager Buzzie Bavasi was orchestrating a different kind of deal. When Robinson contacted him by phone that evening after setting his other plans in motion, Bavasi revealed that the club had done the unthinkable: they had traded Robinson to the New York Giants for a relief pitcher and $35,000.

Robinson was shocked. Though every player at that time understood that such a trade could happen to him very suddenly, it still hurt to be dealt away. "My impulse was to tell Bavasi that Jackie Robinson was no longer the Dodgers' property to be traded," he wrote later.[19] But Robinson knew that his *Look* deal made that retort impossible. He chose to remain silent about his true plans for the time being. The trade did confirm one thing for him, however: that his decision to leave baseball for the business world had come at exactly the right time.

Giants owner Horace Stoneham telephoned Robinson that night and told him how thrilled he was to have the now-former Dodger in his lineup. Robinson was as honest as he thought he could be: he told Stoneham that he would play for the Giants in 1957 if he played for anyone. Then he asked if news of the trade could possibly be kept out of the press. Impossible, Stoneham replied; too many people knew about it already.

Indeed, the trade story was soon front-page news. Reporters besieged the Robinson home as Brooklynites, already angry at O'Malley's threats to leave the borough, picketed the Dodgers' Montague Street offices. "This is like selling the Brooklyn Battery Tunnel," one fan raged. "They can't do this to us." (A more reflective rooter mused, "It sure will be interesting to see Maglie pitch against Robinson again.")[20] Alston, O'Malley, and Bavasi sent Robinson letters praising his "spirit and team play" and hinting at a future job within the organization. Dodgers and Giants players alike spoke in tribute to his competitive fire.

A few days before the *Look* article was to break, rumors about Robinson's true plans leaked out. The magazine's editors called him back to New York from Los Angeles, where he and the family were visiting (and trying to avoid the media), and hastily organized a press conference where he announced his retirement from baseball and his new job with Chock full o'Nuts. After a few polite questions, the knives came out: "Didn't you lie to your friends?" Robinson was asked. "I did not lie," he insisted.[21]

Suddenly, many of the same people who had been lauding Robinson turned on him. Selling his retirement story, and then holding back the truth, struck some as a money-grubbing move. O'Malley called Robinson a mercenary. Stoneham, still hoping to entice Robinson onto his roster, offered him a $60,000 one-year contract. Bavasi predicted that he would take *Look*'s money and then sign with the Giants anyway, thus having his cake, eating it too, and getting paid on both ends of the deal. Robinson was stung by the criticism, especially Bavasi's—which hurt all the more since he had, in fact, considered doing just that.[22] In the end he decided to honor the agreement he had made with Black. He returned the Giants contract to the team unsigned and wrote a businesslike letter to Stoneham explaining that he was going to stick with his original plan to retire. Stoneham responded with a handwritten note wishing Robinson well, along with the wistful sentiment of a true baseball fan: "I can't help thinking it would have been fun to have had you on our side for a year or two."[23]

NOTES

1. Roger Kahn, *The Boys of Summer* (New York: Perennial Library, 1987), p. 406.

2. Sharon Robinson, *Stealing Home* (New York: HarperPerennial, 1997), p. 22.

3. Jackie Robinson, "A Kentucky Colonel Kept Me in Baseball," *Look*, February 8 1955, pp. 82–90.

4. Carl Erskine, *What I Learned From Jackie Robinson* (New York: McGraw-Hill, 2005), pp. 79–80.

5. *Pittsburgh Courier*, September 10, 1955. Cited in Arnold Rampersad, *Jackie Robinson: A Biography* (New York: Ballantine Books, 1998), p. 284.

6. Erskine, *What I Learned From Jackie Robinson*, p. 80.

7. John Drebinger, "Yanks Win First; Collins' 2 Homers Beat Dodgers, 6-5," *New York Times*, September 29, 1955, p. 1.

8. Jackie Robinson, *I Never Had It Made* (New York: Ecco, 1995), p. 120.

9. John Drebinger, "Yanks Top Brooks Behind Byrne, 4-2, For Second In Row," *New York Times*, September 30, 1955, p. 1.

10. Pete Hamill, "The Year of Years," *New York Daily News*, October 9, 2005, pp. 100–103.

11. Robinson, *I Never Had It Made*, p. 120.

12. A.S. "Doc" Young, "The Jackie Robinson Era," *Ebony*, November 1955, pp. 152–156.

13. Rachel Robinson, *Jackie Robinson: An Intimate Portrait* (New York: Harry N. Abrams, 1996), p. 133.

14. Rosoe McGowen, "Robinson Accepts Dodgers' Terms; Yankees Sign Mantle," *New York Times*, January 25, 1956, p. 37.

15. Alvin Maurer, "Jersey City: Remember the Dodgers?" *New York Times*, March 8, 1977, p. 426.

16. *Pittsburgh Courier*, June 23, 1956. Cited in Rampersad, *Jackie Robinson*, p. 295.

17. Rampersad, *Jackie Robinson*, p. 301.

18. Robinson, *Jackie Robinson: An Intimate Portrait*, p. 167.

19. Robinson, *I Never Had It Made*, p. 121.

20. "Brooklyn's Fans Rocked By Trade," *New York Times*, December 14, 1956, p. 46.

21. Kahn, *The Boys of Summer*, p. 389.

22. Robinson, *I Never Had It Made*, p. 122.

23. Carl T. Rowan with Jackie Robinson, *Wait Till Next Year* (New York: Random House, 1960), p. 289.

Chapter 9

BUSINESS AND POLITICS, 1957–1962

While all the fuss about his retirement was raging, Robinson moved to fill his newly freed time with projects that were important to him. As the most recent recipient of the Springarn Medal, he volunteered to help the NAACP with its annual Fight for Freedom Fund campaign.

The Fight for Freedom Fund aimed to raise one million dollars per year for the NAACP's anti-segregation efforts. The group had set the ambitious goal of ending Jim Crow laws in time for the centennial of the Emancipation Proclamation on January 1, 1963. Since the fund's beginnings in 1953, it had never quite made its million-dollar target. Robinson set his sights on achieving this goal in 1957, when he was named the effort's national chairman. At a January 17 press conference, while the controversy over his trade/retirement was still in the news, Robinson made headlines when he announced his Fight for Freedom Fund work and showed off the $10,000 check that William Black, his new employer, had already donated to the cause.

Before he started at Chock full o'Nuts in early March, Robinson took a whirlwind cross-country speaking tour on behalf of the Fight for Freedom Fund. A top NAACP aide, Franklin Williams, was assigned to travel with him. Williams, an excellent fundraiser in his own right, was impressed with Robinson's energy, his easy command of the stage, and his absolute commitment to the cause. The tour schedule included stops in Baltimore, Pittsburgh, Cleveland, Detroit, Cincinnati, St. Louis, San Francisco, Los Angeles, Boston, Philadelphia, and Atlanta. In city after city Robinson held crowds rapt, worked rooms, posed for pictures, even sold kisses to the ladies—whatever he could think of to add to the fund. Robinson knew little about NAACP history, so during their train rides Williams passed on his considerable knowledge. Robinson, a quick study, never failed to work these facts into his speeches. Almost every time Robinson and Williams gave their pitches, their listeners would spontaneously come forward to contribute money from their pockets to the cause. Robinson would remember these outpourings of solidarity and support as being some of the most gratifying experiences of his career.[1]

Starting over as a businessman was a new challenge that Robinson took on with his usual intense enthusiasm, and his new boss was a man he respected. William Black, a Russian immigrant, had built his business from the ground up, starting in the 1920s with a single stand that sold premium roasted nuts in New York City's Times Square. He expanded the concept into a chain of small stores, but during the Depression business plummeted. Black figured that people might not have the money for specialty nuts, but they would always have change for a cup of coffee. He switched gears and transformed his stores into coffee shops. The Chock full o'Nuts chain offered quick service, good coffee, and inexpensive but filling snacks like cream-cheese sandwiches on nut bread and whole-wheat doughnuts. It was a winning combination, and Black soon had outlets throughout the city and surrounding area.

By 1957, Chock full o'Nuts had about 1,000 employees in its 27 shops and coffee-roasting plant. Black was a paternalistic employer who provided a health-care plan, life insurance, a pension program, paid vacations, Christmas bonuses, and a paid day off on each employee's birthday. The trade-off was that he was firmly anti-union. At the time of Robinson's hiring, pro-union sentiment was growing among the chain's mostly black employees, and Black hoped that his new director of personnel would be able to help defuse this potential conflict.

Robinson started his work at "Chock," as he would call it, by visiting the employees at the company's various workplaces. Many of them were baseball fans and welcomed him with excitement. He opened his door to them and was available to help them in any way he could. "His role had few boundaries," Rachel would say. "He represented one employee in court, defended another employee trapped by loan sharks, and attended weddings and funerals."[2] In his time with the company, he would establish employee training programs, oversee company picnics and blood drives, encourage entry-level workers to move up to management, and even run a summer camp for them and their children. Only one thing was difficult for him. "The day when I had the worst butterflies in my stomach, far worse than I ever had with the Dodgers, was when I had to fire an employee," Robinson admitted. "It was necessary as a last resort...But I felt like the governor who sends a man to the electric chair even though he believes that the verdict of the jury and the judge's sentence were just."[3]

One of the most attractive points of the job at Chock full o'Nuts was the boss's support of the civil rights cause. As long as Robinson continued to perform his responsibilities for the company, Black promised to give him all the time he needed to devote to the NAACP and other civil rights groups.[4]

Robinson took full advantage of Black's sympathy. His new position with the NAACP, combined of course with his baseball fame, vaulted him suddenly into a position as a premier spokesman for his race. In April, for example, he appeared on the political interview television show *Meet the Press* to discuss civil rights, and his activities were regularly covered by the media. The attention, combined with Robinson's energy, enabled the Fight for Freedom Fund to reach its million-dollar goal for the first time in 1957.

His worries, however, he kept to himself. Some time that spring, according to Rachel, Robinson saw a doctor about his sudden weight loss and unquenchable thirst. She was "sick at heart" to hear the diagnosis she feared: diabetes. Her husband, on the other hand, was "completely stoic, betraying no sign of emotion" as he listened to his physician describe the disease's frightening consequences. Diabetes meant an increased likelihood of heart attack or stroke. It could lead to kidney failure, blindness, or the loss of a limb. At the time, diabetes was much less well understood than it is today, and it was more difficult to manage. Robinson, whose independence was so important to him, took matters into his own hands. Immediately he swore off the sweets he had always loved and learned how to inject himself with insulin, practicing with a syringe and a tomato until he got it right. In this way he was able to travel, work, and keep his condition private for several more years.[5]

He did, however, confide in his old friend Jack Gordon. "He said that the doctor had told him that for someone who had played sports for so long and didn't smoke or drink, he had never seen a body so badly deteriorated," Gordon would recall.[6] The pressure and the stress of his years in baseball had taken their toll.

LIFE IN THE SUBURBS

When the baseball season began, Robinson found that he didn't miss it at all. The rhythms and routines of suburban life had their own joys. He relished the chance to have dinner each night with Rachel and the children. He liked keeping the expansive lawn neatly clipped, ready for the neighborhood kids to come play softball in the spring and touch football in the fall. He even found a way to enjoy his daily drive to Manhattan and back: he gamed the traffic patterns the way he used to study opposing pitchers and competed with himself to top his best time.

That summer, the closest Robinson got to baseball was serving as a coach for Jackie Junior's Little League team, the Stamford Lions. The ten-year-old was a naturally talented athlete and known as a daredevil among his friends. But in his father's presence, Jackie Junior tended to be shy and withdrawn. Rachel would come to believe that her eldest son's name set him up to be in competition with his famous father—a competition that the boy could not hope to win.

It is also true that the children were set apart from very early on. In their neighborhood and in their schools, they were the only black faces in a sea of white. At this time integration was the ideal for upwardly mobile blacks like the Robinsons, but the day-to-day reality of being a social pioneer was hard on a sensitive child like Jackie Junior. He began to have difficulty keeping up with schoolwork. Only later did his parents suspect an undiagnosed learning disability; at the time they only exhorted him to work harder, which served to discourage Jackie further. Sharon was her father's little princess, enjoying shopping trips and city outings with him; David, the most outdoorsy of the three, loved to fish with his dad and later would spend hours on the golf course with him as a caddy. The relationship between the two Jacks, however, was always fraught.

POLITICAL WORLD

All during the spring and summer, Robinson continued his Fight for Freedom Fund work with speaking engagements around the country, devoting almost every weekend to the cause. He also began exchanging letters with Vice President Richard Nixon as both men monitored the progress of the bill that would become the Civil Rights Act of 1957, the first such piece of legislation to pass Congress since the Reconstruction period nearly a century before. Nixon, a fellow Californian and a huge sports fan, had met Robinson briefly in the early 1950s and had impressed the athlete mightily with his precise recall of a football play Robinson had made for UCLA. In their correspondence Nixon agreed with Robinson that "guaranteeing equal opportunity for all Americans" was indeed an "important objective." Robinson, who pointed out that he was neither a Republican nor a Democrat, was heartened by the law's passage, which had been vociferously opposed by southern Democrats. A few weeks later Robinson was further encouraged by the Eisenhower administration's support of school integration at Little Rock, Arkansas, when the president sent federal troops to protect the nine black students who enrolled at Central High School in September.[7]

Back in the baseball world, it was becoming obvious that neither the Dodgers nor the Giants were long for New York City. On October 8 the Brooklyn ballclub made it official: they would be known as the Los Angeles Dodgers beginning with the 1958 season. Their home field for the first few years would be none other than the Los Angeles Coliseum, site of Jackie Robinson's triumphs as a UCLA Bruin. (The coincidence gave rise to the unsubstantiated rumor that Robinson's 1956 trade was a matter of spite on the part of O'Malley, who could not bear to bring Robinson's career full circle by taking him home to be Los Angeles's hero once again.)

The Dodgers' departure didn't faze Robinson in the least. He was far more concerned with the business and political spheres in which he had fully immersed himself. At times he was able to combine the two, as when he spoke at the American Management Association conference, a gathering for personnel professionals, and challenged the attendees to end race-based hiring biases. Perhaps thinking of his brother Mack, he said it was "undemocratic" to hire college-educated blacks for menial positions, as was still all too often the case. "Those of you who deliberately seek workers first from the so-called majority group and give the minority group a 'break' only as a last resort...become the best advertisement for communism," he said.[8]

In December Robinson wrapped up his Fight for Freedom Fund efforts with a formal $100-a-plate dinner in New York City. More than 1,500 supporters attended to cap off his successful year of fundraising. In thanks, he was elected to the NAACP board, a position he would hold for nearly a decade.

Robinson's first year out of baseball set a pattern he would follow for some time to come. As one of the NAACP's most frequently requested speakers, he continued to travel nationwide to appear at functions for the organization's local chapters. He also remained involved with the Harlem YMCA; fresh from his NAACP fundraising efforts, in 1958 he launched into a drive to raise money for the Y. In politics Robinson made his voice heard at the city, state, and national levels, lobbying for a New York City housing anti-discrimination law and the state's Fair Housing Bill. Some even speculated he might run for office himself. His work at Chock full o'Nuts was also absorbing: the employees voted the union proposal down, and a subsequent lawsuit alleging that Robinson improperly interfered with the process was found to be baseless.

SPEAKING OUT

The issue of school integration was especially close to Robinson's heart. When the White House refused to participate in a conference on the issue proposed by civil rights advocates, Robinson was upset. In a case like this, he was beginning to feel, the NAACP's cautious work-within-the-system approach to social change was inadequate. The tactics espoused by Dr. Martin Luther King Jr. and his newly formed Southern Christian Leadership Conference (SCLC)—civil disobedience and passive resistance—made more sense to him, even though they were provoking violent reactions from segregationists. When labor leader A. Philip Randolph proposed a march in Washington, DC to grab attention for the school integration issue, Robinson jumped on board, even though the NAACP did not officially support it. Characteristically, he was going to go his own way.

The Youth March for Integrated Schools attracted 10,000 demonstrators, many of them college students, to the nation's capital on October 25, 1958. Robinson was designated the march's marshal and led the crowd down Constitution Avenue to the Lincoln Memorial. He was accompanied by Rachel and Jackie Junior, Randolph, singer/actor Harry Belafonte, and Coretta Scott King, Dr. King's wife. A follow-up march was arranged for April 18, 1959. This one, which the NAACP co-sponsored, brought 30,000 demonstrators to Washington and drew words of support from President Eisenhower.

Robinson gained a new outlet for his interests and concerns with the January 1959 launch of "The Jackie Robinson Show" on a local New York radio station. The program, which aired on Sundays at 6:30 P.M., included discussions of current events with such guests as Eleanor Roosevelt, New York City mayor Robert Wagner, and the governor of Connecticut, Abraham Ribicoff.

His potential audience expanded when he began an opinion column in a widely circulated tabloid, the *New York Post*. The column ran three times a week in the sports section, but it was not limited to athletics: Robinson also intended to use the column as a forum for his views on politics and current events. While a ghostwriter, William Branch, helped put the words in publishable form, the ideas were all Robinson's. From a vivid description of a recent lynching in Mississippi to a call to integrate the Professional Golfers' Association, the "Jackie Robinson" column was a fair reflection of its namesake's thoughts and opinions. It made history by becoming the first nationally syndicated op-ed column by a black writer.

The column first edged into national politics in May, when Robinson promised his readers he would investigate the candidates for the 1960 presidential election and share his conclusions in print. Robinson was a registered independent, though he could probably be characterized as a liberal Republican: he was pro-civil rights, but also pro-business and staunchly anti-communist. He made a point of noting that party was of no importance to him compared to the issue of civil rights. His goal was to influence both the Democrats' and the Republicans' choice of a presidential candidate, and throughout 1959 his column returned again and again to the potential nominees and their attitudes on racial equality.

In the summer Robinson came down firmly in favor of Senator Hubert Humphrey of Minnesota for the Democratic nomination. Humphrey was a longtime civil rights advocate who had argued since the late 1940s that the Democrats should take a stand against Jim Crow. After hearing him speak at the Harlem YMCA and at the annual NAACP convention, Robinson was convinced that Humphrey saw, as he did, that civil rights was a question of basic morality. "This man and his principles must be supported," he wrote. "Humphrey's is the kind of leadership that brings pride and inspiration to people in all walks of life."[9] There were no outright civil-rights champions on the Republican side, however. The two leading candidates were Governor Nelson Rockefeller of New York and the sitting vice president, Richard Nixon.

At home, meanwhile, the family was undergoing some major changes. With little David in school full time, Rachel began taking classes at New York University (NYU) in pursuit of a graduate degree in psychiatric nursing. She had always intended to continue her education and return to the work world one day, but her husband had initially opposed this move. Proud as Robinson was of his wife's intelligence, he was equally proud of his own ability to support the family. Inevitably a graduate degree for Rachel would turn into a job for her. Robinson remembered how challenging his own childhood had been, growing up in a home without his mother there full-time, and he did not want that for Jackie, Sharon, and David.

Rachel, however, was firm. "I needed greater freedom to develop personally and professionally," she would say later. "Work and service had contributed to my self-esteem from a very early age." Ever practical, Rachel also realized that she had to prepare to become the family breadwinner one day. The diabetes that was slowly weakening her husband would, in all likelihood, take his life prematurely.[10]

To help manage the household while Rachel was absorbed with schoolwork, her mother Zellee came to live with the family. Rachel's grandmother had died recently, loosening Zellee's ties to California. She settled comfortably into her own suite within the Robinsons' house. Zellee's presence did much to calm Robinson's worries about the new arrangement. Soon he even found a way to enjoy parts of the new routine. "When I had night classes," Rachel remembered, "Jack would wait for me at the Chock full o'Nuts store nearest the Washington Square campus." It reminded them both of their courtship, when they were attending UCLA together.[11]

Robinson's own travel continued unabated. One trip in particular made headlines when he publicly challenged Jim Crow. Robinson was passing through the Greenville, South Carolina airport on October 25, heading to a local NAACP event where he was scheduled to speak. After learning that his welcoming party had been forcibly ejected from the airport's main waiting room, which was reserved for whites, he was outraged. Robinson gave his speech before a jam-packed room and then returned to the airport for his flight home—and for a piece of civil disobedience. Along with two other NAACP members, he headed straight for the "white" waiting room and sat down.

Immediately the three men were approached by a gun-toting security guard.[12] When they refused to move, the airport manager and then a uniformed police officer came to give the same order. Robinson argued that the airport, as a federally subsidized operation, was required to be integrated. This seemed to stump the authorities, and Robinson remained in the waiting room until his flight departed.

This was a small act of defiance, to be sure, but it was heartening for local activists, who soon planned a follow-up demonstration. On New Year's Day 1960—the 97th anniversary of the Emancipation Proclamation—15 black protesters walked into the airport's main waiting room to face the 150 whites, at least half of them police officers, who were there to stop them. More than 250 other protesters remained outside the building, praying and singing in the cold sleet. The demonstration was a peaceful one, just another step on the long road to equality. A month later it was followed by the lunch-counter sit-ins in Greensboro, North Carolina, which would in turn inspire loosely organized sit-ins and demonstrations, mostly by college students, throughout the South. Quietly, Robinson raised money to support the "sit-in kids" who had been jailed.

PRESIDENTIAL POLITICS

As this grass-roots movement gathered steam, the national political parties were gearing up for their presidential primaries. Nelson Rockefeller had dropped out of the Republican race for the nomination, leaving Nixon as the likely Republican nominee. Robinson noted in his column that in his personal correspondence and dealings with the vice president, "generally I've liked what I've seen and heard." He was well aware that much of the black community was suspicious of Nixon and unhappy with the foot-dragging of the Eisenhower administration. Robinson, however, believed Nixon's private assurances that he favored civil rights and wished for more federal action. Black voters had given their monolithic support to Democrat candidates for too long, Robinson argued, making it all too easy for politicians to ignore their needs. "If it should come to a choice between a weak and indecisive Democratic nominee and Vice-President Nixon," Robinson wrote, "I, for one, would enthusiastically support Nixon."[13]

Of all the candidates, however, Robinson still was most enamored of Hubert Humphrey, who was battling Senator John F. Kennedy of Massachusetts for the Democratic nomination. Robinson had already developed a deep distrust of Kennedy, who had made friendly overtures to segregationist southern politicians and who had helped his fellow Democrats temporarily block passage of the Civil Rights Bill of 1957. In February Robinson offered his personal help to Humphrey, who also counted William Black as a supporter. Robinson appeared at the candidate's office opening in Washington, DC and flew to Milwaukee to campaign with him before the Wisconsin state primary.

Humphrey was fighting an uphill battle, however. Kennedy beat him in Wisconsin and then in West Virginia, knocking Humphrey out of the race. As the primary season wound down, it seemed clear that Kennedy would be the Democrats' presidential nominee. Robinson, in his column, continued to disparage the senator's civil-rights record, often in the strongest possible terms: "As long as he continues to play politics at the expense of 18,000,000 Negro Americans, then I repeat: Sen. Kennedy is not fit to be the President of the U.S."[14]

Once the primaries were over, the Kennedy campaign reached out to Robinson directly, inviting him to a face-to-face meeting with the senator. Their talk did not go well. Kennedy "couldn't or wouldn't look me in the eye," Robinson wrote several years later. His mother, Mallie, had always warned him to be wary of those who will not meet your gaze. As the conversation went on, Robinson was struck by how little Kennedy seemed to know about black Americans and their struggle for civil rights. He could not understand how a national political figure could possibly be "so uneducated about the number-one domestic issue of our time."[15]

After their meeting, Kennedy wrote a letter to Robinson that both of them made public. In it he wrote, "If anyone expects the next Democratic Administration to betray the cause of human rights, he can look elsewhere for leadership." News coverage of the letter quoted Robinson, who said that he was "impressed with what appeared to be a sincere effort on the part of Senator Kennedy to let us know he will do something on civil rights if he is elected."[16] But in the end it was not enough. When Lyndon Baines Johnson of Texas, whom Robinson regarded as a firm segregationist, was chosen to be Kennedy's running mate, Robinson threw his support to Richard Nixon. It was a decision Robinson would come to regret.

In the first week of September, Robinson put himself at the disposal of Nixon's presidential campaign. He took an unpaid leave of absence from Chock full o'Nuts to do so: William Black, who had been willing to support all of Robinson's previous political activities, would not underwrite his employee's work for Nixon. Robinson also took a leave from his *New York Post* column. The newspaper, editorially liberal, had received a flood of angry mail about Robinson's endorsement of the Republican. Many of the letters chided Robinson for his one-issue politics, a point that made him furious. Racial equality, to him, was what mattered. "There are pressure groups working" on plenty of issues, Robinson would say. "I'm a pressure group for civil rights."[17]

Robinson's work for the Nixon campaign took him from Brooklyn to Memphis to the West Coast and back. As an unpaid volunteer, his dedication was notable. Everywhere he went, he praised Nixon for the progress that had been made during the eight years of the Eisenhower administration, from the *Brown* decision to the 1957 Civil Rights Act. At the same time he would criticize Kennedy, telling black audiences that the senator "wants us to put him in office so he can learn about us there."[18]

His confidence in the candidate was badly shaken, however, when Martin Luther King was thrown into a Georgia jail on dubious charges in October. Behind the scenes Robinson pleaded with Nixon and his aides to do something on King's behalf, or at least to make a public statement of support and concern. But Nixon did nothing.[19] Stung by his obvious lack of influence within the campaign, Robinson felt humiliated when it was Kennedy who telephoned Coretta Scott King with his sympathies, and when Kennedy's brother Bobby pulled strings to get King released from jail.

Robinson came close to quitting the Nixon campaign at that point, but he chose to honor his commitment rather than switch sides at the last moment. The King episode swung the black vote firmly into the Democratic column. It was a critical factor in Kennedy's razor-thin victory over Nixon on Election Day.

The election of 1960 would have troubling repercussions for the rest of Robinson's life. The most immediate effect was that it got him fired from his *New York Post* column. It wasn't that Robinson had supported

Nixon, the editor-in-chief insisted (not, to Robinson, very convincingly); it was that the columnist hadn't allowed the *Post* itself to break this news. In an embarrassing breach of journalistic form, Robinson had somehow allowed the *New York Times* to find out about it first. Whatever the true motives, the loss of his column left Robinson without a forum to explain the political choices he made, and his reputation suffered.

Robinson returned to work at Chock full o'Nuts and, more tentatively, returned to politics, too. Just days after the election he wrote to New York's Governor Rockefeller, making overtures to a Republican who might yet be a true champion of civil rights. Better still, he returned home. Rachel had been supportive of him during the election odyssey, though she had strongly disagreed with his ultimate choice of a candidate. "As a third-generation Democrat," she admitted, "it pained me to see him cross over into alien and conservative territory."[20]

While he was embroiled in the world of politics, Rachel had temporarily left NYU. The children needed more stability and support at home than a grandmother and a part-time mother could provide. This was especially true of Jackie Junior, who had started classes at Stamford High School in September. Now nearly 14, he was having more difficulty in school than ever. He quit baseball, although he had played on organized teams for years, and while he showed promise in football, he quickly lost interest in that as well. The family reassured themselves with the idea that, like many young teenagers, Jackie was struggling to "find himself."

In the spring of 1961, Robinson helped the NAACP with a new voter-registration drive in the South and was heartened when the Kennedy administration took some bold stands on the enforcement of new anti-Jim Crow laws. He took great interest in the newer civil rights groups that were gaining strength or springing up from the sit-in movement, such as Dr. King's SCLC and the Congress of Racial Equality, or CORE, whose Freedom Rides directly challenged segregation laws. The NAACP looked increasingly staid and ineffective by comparison.

Robinson looked on proudly that May when Rachel earned her master's degree in psychiatric nursing from NYU. A few weeks later she started a full-time job with an experimental program connected with the Albert Einstein College of Medicine in the Bronx, New York. Rachel was part of a team that treated mentally ill individuals on an outpatient basis. The program included support and education for families, who would then continue to help the patients at home. The work was exciting for Rachel, and she quickly moved up in the organization. Soon she became the head of psychiatric nursing at the college.

Jackie Junior was given a fresh start, too. After consulting with a child psychologist, the Robinsons decided to send him to a boarding school in Massachusetts. The Stockbridge School had a good reputation for working with disaffected students, and their son seemed to them to be happy there—happier, at least, than he had been in public school in Stamford.

January of 1962 marked the fifth anniversary of Robinson's retirement from baseball. It was a personal milestone for him, but it was a landmark date for the game, too. Ballplayers become eligible for election to the National Baseball Hall of Fame five years after playing their final season. The voting is done in January of each year, and this would be the first year of Robinson's eligibility—the first chance that the Hall of Fame voters would ever have to add a black man to the baseball pantheon at Cooperstown, New York.

Hall of Fame status was, as Rachel put it, "the prize he most coveted and agonized over."[21] The voters, all members of the Baseball Writers' Association, were some of the very people Robinson had most rankled during his playing days. His recent political activities, too, were bound to have rubbed some of them the wrong way. Elevation to the Hall of Fame would vindicate the pain, the threats, and the insults he had endured. It would be baseball's acknowledgment that Branch Rickey had been right. But he could not count on it, so Robinson braced himself for rejection.

When the phone rang at 103 Cascade Road on the evening of January 23, 1962, Rachel got to it first. Her shriek of joy told Robinson all he needed to know: he was in. He had received votes on 124 of the writers' 160 ballots, four votes over the 75 percent necessary for election to the Hall. "Everybody wanted to hear my reaction," he wrote later. "Truthfully, after having steeled myself to be passed over and not to let it hurt me a lot, I was almost inarticulate."[22]

NOTES

1. Jackie Robinson, *I Never Had It Made* (New York: Ecco, 1995), pp. 128–129.

2. Rachel Robinson, *Jackie Robinson: An Intimate Portrait* (New York: Harry N. Abrams, 1996), p. 155.

3. William R. Conklin, "Jackie Robinson Chock Full o'Poise as Executive," *New York Times*, March 9, 1958, p. S4.

4. Robinson, *I Never Had It Made*, p. 126.

5. Robinson, *Intimate Portrait*, p. 142. It is not clear when Robinson was first diagnosed with diabetes. Some sources maintain that he knew about his condition during his playing days but kept it quiet. For example, see David Falkner, *Great Time Coming: The Life of Jackie Robinson from Baseball to Birmingham* (New York: Simon and Schuster, 1995), p. 229.

6. Arnold Rampersad, *Jackie Robinson: A Biography* (New York: Ballantine Books, 1998), p. 320.

7. Falkner, *Great Time Coming*, pp. 261–263.

8. "Robinson Urges Equality in Jobs," *New York Times*, September 24, 1957, p. 57.

9. Jackie Robinson, "Jackie Robinson," *New York Post*, August 3, 1959, p. 48.

10. Robinson, *Jackie Robinson*, pp. 146–147.

11. Robinson, *Jackie Robinson*, p. 161.

12. "Robinson In Incident," *New York Times*, October 26, 1959, p. 34; Rampersad, *Jackie Robinson: A Biography*, p. 342.

13. Jackie Robinson, "Jackie Robinson," *New York Post*, December 30, 1959, p. 40.

14. Jackie Robinson, "Jackie Robinson," *New York Post*, June 3, 1960, p. 96.

15. Robinson, *I Never Had It Made*, pp. 137–138.

16. Anthony Lewis, "Kennedy Pledges to Stand Firm In Support of Negroes' Rights," *New York Times*, July 2, 1960, p. 6.

17. Roger Kahn, *The Boys of Summer* (New York: Perennial Library, 1987), p. 398.

18. *Dayton Journal*, October 29, 1960. Cited in Rampersad, *Jackie Robinson*, p. 349.

19. Robinson, *I Never Had It Made*, p. 139.

20. Robinson, *Jackie Robinson*, p. 175.

21. Robinson, *Jackie Robinson*, p. 167.

22. Robinson, *I Never Had It Made*, p. 144.

Chapter 10

HALL OF FAMER, 1962–1968

Robinson called his mother and Branch Rickey to share the good news. He knew that being selected for the Baseball Hall of Fame in a player's first year of eligibility was a rare honor; before this year, it had occurred only once. In 1962, both Robinson and Cleveland Indians pitcher Bob Feller made it into the Hall of Fame the first year they possibly could. Robinson didn't even mind that Feller received more votes than he had. (Subsequently, many writers took pleasure in dredging up Feller's 1945 opinion that his future Hall of Fame classmate would never succeed in big-league ball.)[1]

The soon-to-be Hall of Famer returned to print that same month with a regular column in the *Amsterdam News*, a Harlem-based newspaper. Robinson wrote it with the help of Al Duckett, a writer who also worked with Martin Luther King, Jr. The new column appeared on the editorial page and focused squarely on politics.

Robinson used his column as a bullhorn for his views, which were just as strong as ever. When he critiqued President Kennedy for ignoring civil rights in the annual State of the Union address, or when he described the demonstrations and voter-registration efforts in Albany, Georgia that would come to be known as the Albany Movement, Robinson's new readers seemed to appreciate his point of view. But when he took on the anti-Semitism that was beginning to creep into the rhetoric of some black protesters, his opinion wasn't as well received.

"BLACK SUPREMACY IS JUST AS BAD
AS WHITE SUPREMACY"

At issue was a fast-food restaurant that was to open on Harlem's 125th Street. The restaurant space was owned by Frank Schiffman, proprietor of the famous Apollo Theater. Schiffman leased the space to Sol Singer, the owner of a fast-food chain. But the new restaurant would mean competition for an existing black-owned establishment nearby, and both Schiffman and Singer were Jewish. For several weeks a group of activists led by Lewis Micheaux, a member of the radical African Nationalist movement, had been picketing the Apollo, chanting "Black man must stay; Jew must go!"

Robinson's column on the matter sharply criticized Micheaux and his group. He noted that the space had been available for some time, and that no black businesses had stepped forward to rent it. What offended him most, however, was the notion that black people, who had been oppressed for so long, would use tools of prejudice and bigotry against others. "Anti-Semitism is as rotten as anti-Negroism," he wrote.[2]

The day after the column was published, Micheaux threatened to picket the Chock full o'Nuts shop on 125th Street unless Robinson retracted his assertions. Robinson refused. "All my life we have been fighting against this same thing as it applies to the Negro," he said. "I won't retract something like this...Black supremacy is just as bad as white supremacy."[3]

On July 14, the picketing of the Chock full o'Nuts outlet began, with signs such as "Jackie is a classified so called Negro" and "The Jackie of all trades and master of only one. His mouth is too big." Robinson received messages of support from Roy Wilkins of the NAACP, Whitney Young of the National Urban League, representatives of the Anti-Defamation League, and others, but the demonstrations went on for four days. The chairman of the State Commission on Human Rights began to make noise about getting involved. Finally, Robinson and Micheaux came together on a local radio program and battled on the air. They argued for an hour that began with accusations and quickly degenerated into name-calling, as Micheaux called Robinson "a flunky for whites" and Robinson dismissed Micheaux as "a bigot, a demagogue."[4]

Somehow, once all the insults had been traded, the two men agreed that anti-Semitism had no place in the fight for black rights. Two days later Micheaux was an honored guest at a testimonial dinner in Robinson's honor. He sat at Frank Schiffman's table.

The dinner, which had been planned to coincide with the Hall of Fame induction ceremonies that were set for the next week, was a high point for Robinson. It was sponsored by Martin Luther King's SCLC, and its proceeds went to the organization, which was in the midst of leading the Albany Movement and in dire need of funds. More than 900 people, including Governor Nelson Rockefeller, Roy Wilkins, Ralph Bunche, Ed Sullivan, and boxer Floyd Patterson, attended the event at the Waldorf-Astoria Hotel in New York. Dr. King had had to remain in Albany, but an aide read a message from him that thanked Robinson for his courage in championing equal rights for all people, black and white. Robinson, who admired King deeply, was overcome. Congratulatory telegrams were read from President Kennedy and Vice President Johnson, among others.[5]

MAKING HISTORY, AGAIN

Monday, July 23 was cool and rainy in Cooperstown, New York, but nothing could dampen Robinson's spirits. The Hall of Fame induction ceremony, for him, was one of the most joyous days of his life.

"I feel quite inadequate to this honor," he said in his prepared remarks. "It is something that could never have happened without three people—Branch Rickey, who was as a father to me; my wife and my mother. They are all here today, making the honor complete. And I don't think I will ever come down from Cloud Nine."[6] After speeches from Feller and the other two inductees, old-timers Bill McKechnie and Edd Roush, fans swarmed the newly minted Hall of Famers on the dais. Robinson behaved like a delighted fan himself, deftly pivoting to capture the moment with a home-movie camera.

A few weeks later, when three black churches were destroyed in suspicious fires near Albany, Georgia, Robinson was there to lend his support. The churches had all participated in the SCLC's voter registration drive. The local sheriff refused to call the burnings arson, nor would he investigate the shots that had been fired at activists and at the homes of black residents. Robinson inspected the still-smoldering ruins of Mount Olive Baptist Church and immediately announced his intention to lead a fundraising effort that would help the congregations rebuild. Over the next two months, he raised $60,000 on their behalf.

Robinson had a serious health scare in early 1963 when an operation on his painfully arthritic left knee led to a raging infection, complicated by his diabetes. He remained in the hospital for weeks, often barely conscious. The family rallied around him; even Jackie Junior, who was back in public school in Stamford after his boarding school kicked him out, was attentive. But when Robinson finally returned home, Jackie disappeared. He cleaned out his savings account and ran away to California with a friend. The Robinsons had no idea how desperately unhappy their son was. Robinson's reaction was something that his wife could never forget: "Jack just crumbled. He started to cry. It was the first time the family—Sharon and David, my mother, all of us—had seen him break down and cry."[7] Two weeks later the Los Angeles police picked Jackie Junior up and sent him back home.

Robinson's physical and emotional recovery from these events was slow, and for several months he remained close to home. But in the spring, as blacks in the South continued to press for voting and education rights and white violence escalated, Robinson was drawn back into the struggle and stepped up his travels once again. He saw himself not as a leader of the movement, but as a supporter, a morale-booster. Several athletes made appearances with him, a development Robinson had long wished for. Patterson became a frequent companion, and baseball's Curt Flood went to Jackson, Mississippi with Robinson to support a black student's enrollment in the University of Mississippi in early 1963.

DANGEROUS TIMES

On several occasions Robinson found himself in threatening situations. One of the most frightening was in May 1963, when Robinson and Patterson traveled to Birmingham, Alabama, where the segregationist sheriff Bull Connor and his men had turned attack dogs and high-pressure hoses on peaceful demonstrators led by Martin Luther King. The incident, which was broadcast on national television, had horrified the nation, but Connor was still using his brutal methods against the protesters, who would not give up.

Wherever the two famous athletes went in Birmingham—their motel, which had been firebombed by white supremacists the day before; a black-owned restaurant, the only place in town that would serve them; rallies where they were cheered by joyful activists—they were tailed by police officers, vigilant for the slightest traffic infraction or most minor altercation that would give an excuse for their arrest. The sense of oppression was intense and constant. Robinson was glad "to give our thanks to the fighting people who were standing fast against fire hoses, police dogs, riot clubs, guns and bombs," as he put it.[8] But he was anguished by how little he could do beyond that.

During his trip to Birmingham, Robinson realized that what King and the SCLC needed most was cash to make bail for the thousands of protesters who were being arrested there. He and Rachel decided to turn their home over to a fundraising effort on their behalf. On June 23, the Robinsons hosted a concert in the natural amphitheater formed by the gently sloping lawn behind their home. Dizzy Gillespie, Dave Brubeck, Duke Ellington, and other nationally known musicians performed; six hundred people attended. The murder of the NAACP's Medgar Evers in Mississippi only 10 days earlier gave those gathered at the event a sense of shared purpose and determination, even as they reveled in the music. More than $15,000 was raised for the SCLC at what the Robinsons billed as an "Afternoon of Jazz." From that point on the Robinsons made the fundraiser an annual event, each year designating a different civil rights group as its beneficiary.

The entire Robinson family attended the historic March on Washington for Jobs and Freedom on August 28, 1963, along with 200,000 other peaceful demonstrators. Dr. King's "I Have a Dream" speech held even the children rapt, and Robinson enjoyed the chance to share this part of his life with them. The sense of unity thrilled them all but was shattered four weeks later by the Birmingham church bombing that killed four young girls as they attended Sunday school. Events like this one made it hard for even firm King supporters like Robinson to suppress thoughts of retaliatory violence.

THE DEBATE WITH MALCOLM X

By now some black leaders, in fact, were openly advocating violent revolt against white oppression. Malcolm X was one of the strongest voices at this radical end of the political spectrum. A leader within the Nation of Islam, commonly known as the Black Muslim movement, Malcolm opposed the goal of integration, instead favoring a system of black separatism, and he was quick to condemn blacks he saw as "sellouts" to wealthy and powerful whites. In November he set his sights on Robinson.

Robinson's *Amsterdam News* column of November 16 was a ringing defense of Ralph Bunche, the American black man who was serving as undersecretary of the United Nations. Bunche had been attacked by Malcolm and by Congressman Adam Clayton Powell of Harlem for his lack of action in the racial struggle within the United States. Robinson argued that, as an official of an international body, Bunche was required to remain apart from such internal issues. Then Robinson went on the offensive against Malcolm, whom he called "a militant on Harlem street corners where militancy is not dangerous" and "a leader who finds himself left by the wayside in the Negro's onward march toward freedom, mainly because he talks the language of the segregationists—a language which the Negro people scorn."[9]

Malcolm's stinging reply to Robinson, published in the *Amsterdam News*, was at first lost in the frenzy of grief that surrounded the assassination of President Kennedy. But when readers caught up to it, they may well have been stunned by his attack on black America's onetime idol. "You became a great baseball player after your White Boss (Mr. Rickey) lifted you to the Major Leagues," Malcolm began, and went on to condemn Robinson for his testimony on Paul Robeson in 1949, his support of Richard Nixon in 1960, his job with William Black, and his warm relationship with Nelson Rockefeller. "Just who are you playing ball for today, good Friend?" Malcolm asked mockingly.[10]

Robinson shot back a defensive column in return. Calling Malcolm's broadside "one of the things I shall cherish" because "coming from you, an attack is a tribute," he wrote: "Personally, I reject your racist views. I reject your dream of a separate state...Negroes are not fooled by your vicious theories that they are dying for freedom to please the white man. Negroes are fighting for freedom and rejecting your racism because we feel our stake in America is worth fighting for."[11]

The argument went almost entirely ignored in the mainstream press, but among blacks it touched some very sensitive nerves. For the rest of Robinson's life, there would always be those in the black community who would whisper "Uncle Tom" behind his back—or even shout it to his face.

LEAVING CHOCK

This controversy certainly did not strengthen Robinson's position within Chock full o'Nuts as his contract with the company drew to a close. His frequent absences from the office had taken a toll on his effectiveness there, and more and more personnel decisions had been made without his input or knowledge. Robinson had been hired because of his stature among blacks in New York City, but the exchange with Malcolm tarnished that image. It became clear to him that his contract would not be renewed, so in a face-saving move, he announced his resignation from the company in February 1964. He was leaving, he said, to join Nelson Rockefeller's bid to become the Republican presidential nominee in the 1964 election. Rockefeller, Robinson explained, was the only Republican in the field who could "make the Democrats live up to some of their promises" on civil rights.[12]

Robinson became a deputy national director of the Rockefeller campaign, though the position was unpaid. He explored a number of business possibilities in 1964 and in the next few years (including an insurance company, a construction firm, and a bank), many of which, he hoped, would also have a role in the cause of racial equality. That spring he published a landmark book on the integration of baseball, *Baseball Has*

Done It. In its pages Robinson shared the story of his early days in the game, as well as in-their-own-words accounts of others involved in the drama, including Branch Rickey, Larry Doby, Don Newcombe, and even his old Philadelphia nemesis Ben Chapman. His purpose, however, was not to produce an oral history, but to send out a call to action. If baseball, a mere game, can overcome the barriers and prejudices of centuries, Robinson asked, why can't the rest of society do the same? He called on black athletes to get involved in the fight. "No Negro in the public eye can shilly-shally any longer," he wrote. "I have been aggressive in defense of civil rights. I shall continue to be aggressive. Aggressiveness has never hurt me in business or in any other way. I may have been denied a few opportunities, but I've balanced accounts in others. And I can live with myself."[13]

Meanwhile, as Robinson campaigned for Rockefeller and continued making appearances at civil-rights events with Martin Luther King and others, 17-year-old Jackie Junior made a momentous decision: he dropped out of high school and signed up for the U.S. Army. He told his mother about his choice "with an air of confidence I hadn't seen in him for a long time," Rachel wrote later. "He said he had a lot of learning to do and needed discipline as well. He had been told the army offered both."[14] Rachel, who believed in education above all, pleaded with him to reconsider. Robinson, however, seemed to agree with his son that the military might provide him some necessary structure.

ANOTHER PRESIDENTIAL RACE

Politics consumed Robinson for much of the year. Rockefeller's brand of Republicanism, while popular in liberal New York, was a minority stance within the Republican Party. The presidential nomination went to Barry Goldwater, a conservative—some might say reactionary—senator from Arizona. Some of Goldwater's support came directly from segregationist Southerners, which made him anathema to Robinson: "In my opinion [Goldwater] is a bigot, an advocate of white supremacy," he wrote in his column.[15]

Robinson attended the Republican national convention in San Francisco in the summer of 1964 as a special delegate and did all he could to influence the platform in a pro-civil rights direction, but that effort failed. When Rockefeller was jeered by Goldwater supporters during his convention-floor speech, Robinson nearly got into a fistfight with another delegate. He returned home convinced that Goldwater was dangerous for the nation as a whole and for black Americans, in particular, and immediately volunteered to campaign for Democrats Lyndon Johnson and Hubert Humphrey, who did win in November. Nonetheless, Robinson stayed active in Republican politics, convinced that blacks had to have a place in both parties if their needs were to be addressed.

Robinson's most important business venture came to fruition in December 1964 with the opening of Freedom National Bank in Harlem. One of the few mostly black-owned banks in the country at the time, Robinson and his partners believed that Freedom was critical for the success of the black community as a whole. Financial institutions had the potential to reinforce civil rights, he felt, if only potential black entrepreneurs would pool their resources and put their capital to work locally, in their own neighborhoods.[16] As the bank's chairman of the board, Robinson was involved in all its major decisions, though financial professionals ran its day-to-day business. His name was still a valuable door-opener, and the bank was supported by nonprofit foundations, labor unions, and many individuals. Martin Luther King opened an account at Freedom and deposited his 1964 Nobel Peace Prize check there.

In 1965 Robinson returned to baseball, after a fashion. The ABC television network was launching the first-ever national baseball broadcast that season and signed Robinson to join its on-air team. This made Robinson a barrier-breaker yet again as the first black network baseball commentator. After years away from baseball and his unhappy exit from it, he had a new perspective on the game's importance to him. "If it hadn't been for sports, I doubt I would have accomplished much in life," he could say now.[17]

He was glad for the distraction during the summer, when Jackie Junior was shipped off to Vietnam after a year of Army training. Americans were only beginning to become aware of the conflict in that southeast Asian nation, as the United States committed more and more troops there in an effort to stave off pro-communist Viet Cong forces. Distance and danger brought father and son closer in some ways; in long letters the two men were able to communicate in ways they were not able to manage while face to face. But the war took a terrible toll on Jackie Junior, who suffered shrapnel wounds in an ambush that killed two other soldiers. The chronic pain led him into drug dependency. His deployment ended with a Purple Heart, an honorable discharge, and a heroin addiction that he managed to keep secret from his family—for a while.

Soon after Robinson received word of his son's injury, he was shaken by news of Branch Rickey's death. "He was one of the kindest, warmest men I ever knew. He was like a father to me," Robinson told the press.[18] What he saw at Rickey's funeral, however, was hard to take: only two other black ballplayers were there to honor the man who had risked so much to open baseball's doors to them. The lack of gratitude, or even recognition, on the part of younger blacks seemed emblematic to Robinson of a generation that was ready to abandon reason and the vote in favor of alienation and street violence. This was the year that the phrase "Black Power" came into vogue and the militant Black Panthers were founded, the year that Malcolm X was assassinated. Even as the pace of peaceful integration quickened in the South, riots exploded in the north. Robinson's hopes for social and economic equality seemed quaint in comparison to the violent rhetoric that was exploding all around him.

WORKING FOR THE GOVERNOR

Robinson's warm relationship with Nelson Rockefeller resulted in a paid position within the governor's administration as a community affairs aide early in 1966. Robinson threw himself into the work: ever the idealist, he truly believed in Rockefeller as a force for good in the political world. The job meant testifying before legislative committees, meeting with community groups, and traveling on Rockefeller's behalf to various gatherings, but as the year went on and Rockefeller's re-election campaign heated up, Robinson took on campaign duties as well. His celebrity status gave him entrée to liberal groups that otherwise would be dead set against a Republican, as well as to conservative groups that otherwise would be dead set against a liberal. One of Robinson's staff members remembered a meeting with a group in Staten Island that was "definitely antiblack . . . but for Jackie, they turned out in droves; the halls were packed, and Jackie was the key. It was like, Okay, okay, enough, we'll vote for Rockefeller—now Jackie, how about that play in that game? They adored him . . . We got the votes." Rockefeller won reelection that fall by a comfortable margin.[19]

Somehow, Robinson also found the energy to appear at civil rights demonstrations, produce his column, continue his work at the bank, and even take on the job of general manager of a professional football team. The Brooklyn Dodgers were introduced in May 1966 as a new team in the one-year-old Continental Football League. The team, which never actually played in Brooklyn, was not a success. It played a few games at the city-owned Downing Stadium on Randalls Island before its financing collapsed in late October. The football Dodgers played the rest of their schedule as a "road club" operated by the league before fading out after their single season ended.

The year of almost frantic activity for Robinson masked the fact that he was becoming politically isolated within the Civil Rights Movement.

In early 1967 that mask fell away when Robinson used his column to sharply criticize two longtime allies, Martin Luther King Jr. and Roy Wilkins of the NAACP. King had begun to speak out against the Vietnam War, a development that Robinson found disturbingly anti-American. Wilkins, Robinson felt, had kept new faces and young blood off the NAACP board, thus making the organization increasingly out of touch. That he lashed out at Wilkins for being too hidebound, and at King for being too radical, was an irony Robinson did not seem to see.

King responded to his old friend's public attack gently, with a long and private telephone call in which he explained his point of view. Wilkins, however, took Robinson to task with a bluntly worded letter. He, for one, was fed up with Robinson's long-held belief that "'because I see it this way I have to say it'... The basis of informed comment is not simple, self-serving personal re-affirmation but truth arrived at through reasoning," Wilkins wrote. "If you had played ball with a hot head instead of a cool brain, you would have remained in the minors."[20]

A YEAR OF TRAGEDY

Jackie Junior left the Army in June 1967 a changed man, but not in the way he had expected. For months he drifted between Colorado, where his old unit was based, and Connecticut, unable to land a job or to remain for long in his family's home. Jackie told his parents that he just needed time to figure things out, and they believed him, despite all the signs that there was something seriously wrong in their son's life. "There is nothing that can blind parents as much as loving hope," Robinson wrote later.[21]

They were completely unprepared, then, when Jackie Junior was arrested in Stamford in March of 1968 for possession of heroin, marijuana, and an illegally concealed gun. Robinson learned the news from a reporter who called him at his office for comment several hours after his son's early-morning arrest. He, Rachel, and Sharon—who heard about her brother's predicament on her car radio—converged on the Stamford police station where he was being held. The press was waiting for them. Both women were in tears, the reporters noted, but Robinson gave them the quotes he knew they needed.

"I guess I had more of an effect on other people's kids than I had on my own," he told them sadly. He sketched the events of Jackie's Army service, his combat injury, and his admitted use of marijuana. But he placed the blame for Jackie's troubles squarely upon himself. "My problem was my inability to spend much time at home," Robinson said. "I guess I thought my family was secure, that at least we wouldn't have anything to worry about, so I went running around everywhere else."[22]

It was now clear to the Robinsons that Jackie Junior needed serious help. Pledging to stand behind him, the family bailed him out of jail and drove him immediately to New Haven, Connecticut. Rachel was now an assistant professor of nursing at Yale University, and she was able to quickly find a place for her son at Yale-New Haven Hospital. A few weeks later a local judge declared Jackie an addict and ordered him into a drug rehabilitation program.

His son's arrest was the first of a series of wrenching events for Robinson that year. While Jackie Junior was still hospitalized, Martin Luther King was assassinated in Memphis, Tennessee. This was something that Robinson and many others had long dreaded and half-expected, but it was still a shock, "the most disturbing and distressing thing we've had to face in a long time," Robinson said.[23] Violence resulted in some cities, but Robinson found himself doing a great deal of soul searching after Dr. King's death. He came to believe that nonviolence, a fine goal, might not be possible in the real world. "There was a time when I deeply believed in America," Robinson wrote a few years after the events of April, 1968. "I have become bitterly disillusioned."[24]

At the end of April, 18-year-old Sharon married her high-school boyfriend, a match that her parents and especially her mother deeply opposed. Despite their misgivings, the Robinsons hosted the wedding and helped their daughter set up a household. But within three months, Sharon had to admit her parents were right: Her husband was physically and emotionally abusive. She moved back into her parents' home and filed for divorce.

Meanwhile, Robinson heard from his brother Edgar in Pasadena that their mother, Mallie, had collapsed in the driveway of 121 Pepper Street, where the extended Robinson family still lived. Robinson flew to California immediately, but it was too late to speak to his mother one last time. By the time he reached her, she was dead.

"I didn't think I could bear to look upon her face," he wrote later. But he managed it. The serenity he saw in Mallie's expression told him everything he needed to know, and more. All her life Mallie had given of herself—her time, her money, her food, her home—to others. Her youngest son had often criticized her selflessness, but now he saw that her outreach was a conscious choice, and that it had given her a deep sense of peace. "In death she was still teaching me how to live," he realized.[25]

The unrelenting stress placed an impossible burden on his diabetes-weakened body, but Robinson only stepped up his schedule. He and Rachel hosted a luncheon at their Stamford home for 70 members of the National Newspaper Publishers Association so that Governor Rockefeller, entering memorably via a helicopter landing on the lawn, could speak to the group. Days later, thousands arrived for the Robinsons' annual Afternoon of Jazz benefit on that same lawn. The proceeds this year went to help support Martin Luther King's young children.

The day after the benefit, Robinson saw his doctor, complaining of nagging chest pains, which turned out to be a heart attack—a mild one, but a warning sign for him. He had to slow down, and not even another round of presidential politics was supposed to rouse him from his recuperation at home.

Robinson could only take his enforced rest for six weeks, however, before inserting himself back into the political world. Richard Nixon was back in the forefront of the Republican Party after Goldwater's massive defeat in 1964. Robinson's misgivings about Nixon at the end of the 1960 campaign had metastasized into near-hatred. Rockefeller had ultimately decided not to pursue the presidency in the 1968 campaign, leaving the way clear for Nixon to grab the nomination. When Nixon named Spiro Agnew of Maryland as his running mate, Robinson broke with the Republicans for good. "The GOP didn't give a damn about my vote or the votes—or welfare—of my people," he decided.[26] Calling the Nixon–Agnew ticket "racist" and predicting riots among blacks if they were elected, he resigned from Rockefeller's staff to campaign for the Democratic nominee, Hubert Humphrey.

Still, Robinson hoped to be reinstated to Rockefeller's team when the election was over. That was not to be, despite a heartfelt letter he wrote to the governor. "If you were Black and searching for dignity," he asked Rockefeller, "could you do any different?"[27]

Few Republican liberals followed Robinson into the Humphrey camp, and once again, he found himself a man alone. There was little he could do to help the Democrat at any rate: Nixon won the election. When the *Amsterdam News* discontinued his opinion column that fall, it seemed Robinson's day as an influential political voice was done.

He tried to be philosophical, to take the long view. "When I quit [baseball] I went in to the NAACP, and the conservatives found me hard to take," Robinson reminisced around this time. "They were men of eighty. Their attitude was: don't rock the boat. Today militants find me hard to take. Their attitude is: burn everything. But I haven't changed much. The times have changed around me."[28]

NOTES

1. Arnold Rampersad, *Jackie Robinson: A Biography* (New York: Ballantine Books, 1998), p. 130. The five-years-after-retirement rule was instituted in 1954. Before that, only one player gained Hall of Fame status as soon as he was eligible. In 1939, Lou Gehrig entered the Hall "by acclamation" immediately after the end of his final season because he was so clearly near death.

2. *New York Amsterdam News*, July 14, 1962. Cited in Rampersad, *Jackie Robinson*, p. 365.

3. "Harlem Pickets Switch Tactics," *New York Times*, July 14, 1962, p. 8.

4. Jackie Robinson, *I Never Had It Made* (New York: Ecco, 1995), p. 150.

5. Robinson, *I Never Had It Made*, p. 144; "900 Attend Tribute to Jackie Robinson," *New York Times*, July 21, 1962, p. 10.

6. Robert M. Lipsyte, "Baseball's Hall of Fame Inducts Robinson, Feller, McKechnie and Roush," *New York Times*, July 24, 1962, p. 20.

7. Rampersad, *Jackie Robinson*, p. 371.

8. Jackie Robinson, *Baseball Has Done It* (Brooklyn, NY: Ig Publishing, 2005), pp. 26–27.

9. Jackie Robinson, "Malcolm X and Adam Powell," *New York Amsterdam News*, November 16, 1963, p. 1.

10. Malcolm X, "Malcolm X's Letter," *New York Amsterdam News*, November 30, 1963, p. 1.

11. Jackie Robinson, "Jackie Robinson Again Writes to Malcolm X," *New York Amsterdam News*, December 14, 1963, p. 1.

12. John F. Murphy, "Jackie Robinson Quits His Job To Aid Rockefeller Campaign," *New York Times*, February 1, 1964, p. 8.

13. Robinson, *Baseball Has Done It*, p. 210.

14. Rachel Robinson, *Jackie Robinson: An Intimate Portrait* (New York: Harry N. Abrams, 1996), p. 194.

15. *New York Amsterdam News*, July 4, 1964. Cited in Rampersad, *Jackie Robinson*, p. 386.

16. Robinson, *I Never Had It Made*, p. 166.

17. *Los Angeles Herald-Examiner*, April 1, 1965. Cited in Rampersad, *Jackie Robinson*, p. 398.

18. "Baseball Leaders Pay Respects To Rickey's Character and Skill," *New York Times*, December 11, 1965, p. 39.

19. Rampersad, *Jackie Robinson*, p. 407.

20. David Falkner, *Great Time Coming: The Life of Jackie Robinson from Baseball to Birmingham* (New York: Simon and Schuster, 1995), pp. 324–325.

21. Robinson, *I Never Had It Made*, p. 217.

22. William Borders, "Jackie Robinson Jr. Is Arrested On Heroin Charge in Stamford," *New York Times*, March 5, 1968, p. 20.

23. Lawrence Van Gelder, "Dismay In Nation," *New York Times*, April 5, 1968, p. 1.

24. Robinson, *I Never Had It Made*, p. 215.

25. Robinson, *I Never Had It Made*, p. 267.

26. Robinson, *I Never Had It Made*, p. 207.

27. Rampersad, *Jackie Robinson*, p. 431.

28. Roger Kahn, *The Boys of Summer* (New York: Perennial Library, 1987), p. 406.

Chapter 11

HEARTBREAK, 1969–1972

Robinson was forced to take the long view when it came to his son's recovery from drug addiction, too. Jackie Junior joined a live-in rehabilitation program called Daytop several weeks after his arrest in March of 1968. The well-regarded program had an excellent track record, partly because it was administered by former addicts who had been through the program themselves. But it was no panacea, and Jackie seemed to take a step backward for each move he made forward. Late in the summer he was arrested again, this time on charges of "loitering for the purposes of prostitution" and threatening a police officer with a gun. He was ordered back into rehab rather than sentenced to jail, but the courts would not look so kindly upon another offense.

Robinson busied himself with various business deals, including a seafood-restaurant franchising company and the Jackie Robinson Construction Corporation, which was established to build low- and middle-income housing in the New York City area. Freedom National Bank took up a substantial amount of his time, too. But the pace of his activities had to slow as diabetes took its insidious toll on his circulation and his vision. Walking was becoming more and more difficult for Robinson, and he was losing his eyesight as well. Rachel's nursing experience made it impossible for her to ignore her husband's deterioration. He was only 50 years old, but she feared that he could not have more than a year or two to live. Quietly, Rachel took a sabbatical from her teaching post at Yale to spend as much time with him as she could.

Sobered by his failing health, Robinson most wanted to produce an autobiography that would put both his playing days and his post-baseball work as an activist into perspective. He and his longtime collaborator, Alfred Duckett, worked on the book for the next two years. It would be published as *I Never Had It Made* in 1972, and it was to Robinson's mind the definitive story of his life.

In the spring of 1970, Robinson made headlines once again when he testified in Curt Flood's antitrust lawsuit against baseball. Flood was fighting baseball's reserve clause, the system that allowed club owners absolute control of the players whose contracts they held. Flood hoped to establish a system of free agency that would allow ballplayers to exercise at least some independent choice. Robinson was one of the few players or former players willing to openly take Flood's side: the two men had done some civil rights work together in the past. Besides, as Robinson said in court, "Anything that is one-sided is wrong in America. The reserve clause is one-sided in favor of the owners and should be modified to give the player some control over his destiny."[1] Flood's suit eventually resulted in the free agency system that baseball employs today.

JACKIE JUNIOR'S ROAD BACK HOME

By this time Jackie Junior seemed fully committed to the Daytop program. His recovery from addiction continued, and soon he would be well enough to help others, too. Robinson turned his activist energies into spreading the anti-drug message, speaking at rallies and lobbying government entities to devote more funds to drug treatment and prevention programs.

The Robinsons hosted a joyful picnic for Jackie and 50 other Daytop residents at their home in the spring of 1970 to thank the group for all they had done for their son. As the guests packed to leave, Robinson wrote later, Jackie hugged his father with the kind of loving affection the two had not shared since he was a small boy. "That single moment paid for every bit of sacrifice, every bit of anguish, I had ever undergone," Robinson wrote. "I had my son back."[2]

Tragically, he would not have Jackie back for long. Barely a year later, on June 17, 1971, Jackie Junior was killed in a car accident on the Merritt Parkway near Stamford. By now a full member of Daytop's staff, he had been hard at work on his parents' annual Afternoon of Jazz, which was set to benefit the organization that he credited with saving his life. The police concluded that he fell asleep at the wheel. His neck broken by the impact, he died almost instantly.

For his family, the grief was nearly unbearable. Rachel, ordinarily so composed, began to scream when she heard the terrible news and could not stop. Robinson broke down and sobbed in friends' arms. It was David, now 18 and a student at Stanford University in California, who became the family's strength. A prose poem he wrote for his brother, "The Baptism," became Jackie Junior's eulogy. "Give me my freedom so that I might fly," he read at the funeral.[3] It was the only comfort his parents could take: that after all the pain of addiction and withdrawal, the horrors of war and the unexpected stresses of his childhood, Jackie was free and could at last fly.

To honor Jackie's memory, the Robinsons held the benefit concert as scheduled, six days after the funeral. Roberta Flack sang, Dave Brubeck and others played, and Rev. Jesse Jackson, whom Robinson had singled out as a bright young star of the Civil Rights Movement, inspired the crowd with his words. Robinson himself spoke briefly to describe his eldest son's dedication to Daytop and the work he had done to make the day possible. More than $40,000 was raised for the program.

PAYING TRIBUTE

In December *Sport* magazine named Robinson its "Man of 25 Years," the most significant athlete of the past quarter-century. A luncheon in New York City gathered some of the greatest names in American sports, including golf's Arnold Palmer, basketball's Bill Russell, and hockey's Gordie Howe, to pay tribute to Robinson's achievements on the field and off. It seemed that appreciation and affection for Robinson's Brooklyn Dodgers, and for Robinson himself, was growing and deepening now. The buzz was building about sportswriter Roger Kahn's soon-to-be-published book *The Boys of Summer,* a poignant look at the Dodgers as they had been during their pennant run and as they were 20 years later. His team was passing into mythic status before Robinson's eyes. The 1972 baseball season would, after all, mark the twenty-fifth anniversary of his major-league debut.

When the Los Angeles Dodgers invited Robinson to attend a pre-game ceremony during the season to retire his uniform number, he resisted at first. The old bitterness was still there. But Walter O'Malley, Robinson's nemesis, was no longer running the team; Peter O'Malley, Walter's son, was the ballclub's president now. Don Newcombe, a teammate with whom Robinson remained close, urged him to come. The Dodgers retired Robinson's number 42 on June 4, 1972, as well as Roy Campanella's number 39 and pitcher Sandy Koufax's number 32. All three Hall of Famers were there to accept the honor.

When old friends came to see Robinson during his visit to Los Angeles, they were stunned to see how frail he had become. Robinson was now completely blind in his right eye, and he could see only dimly with his left. The restricted blood circulation in his legs made walking a painful ordeal. Ray Bartlett, his teammate and buddy from childhood through college, described how Robinson could only move "with difficulty and very slowly. I remembered the days when he was such a tremendous athlete... I felt inside that he was forcing himself to keep going, he had too much determination to stop."[4]

As October and the World Series approached, the commissioner's office was pressed to recognize the anniversary of baseball's integration during the championship week. Robinson was invited to throw out the first pitch of Game Two in Cincinnati's Riverfront Stadium. He came close to refusing, but for two things: he was promised a substantial gift to Daytop if he appeared, and he would be given a nationally broadcast platform to speak his mind for, it would turn out, one last time.

The entire Robinson family—Rachel, Sharon and her second husband, David, and Zellee—was there on the field for the pre-game ceremony. "I am extremely proud and pleased," Robinson said. "I'm going to be tremendously more pleased and more proud when I look at that third base coaching line one day and see a black face managing in baseball."[5]

He was still fighting with all the strength he could muster, but the game's current stars barely noticed. When Robinson was led to the visiting team's locker room before the game began, the Oakland Athletics—black and white players alike—ignored him, almost to a man. They "paid him no attention, were not interested in coming over to greet him," according to Red Barber, the old Dodgers broadcaster. "It is terrible when human beings forget their blessings and forget to say thank you."[6]

If Robinson minded this, he did not mention it to his old teammates Pee Wee Reese and Joe Black, who were with him for the World Series ceremony. The men were making small talk when Robinson casually mentioned that his blindness wasn't his main concern: "I'm gonna go into the hospital and have my leg amputated." Black and Reese were shaken, both by the revelation and by Robinson's calm. "That's just what he said, like he's talking about apples and oranges," Black recalled. "Pee Wee gets real upset, says, 'Can't they do something?' [Jack] says, 'Naw, the sugar— they figure they'd cut it and that would stop [the pain]. And I'll take awhile and get an artificial leg and I'll learn to walk and I'll play golf, and you know what, Pee Wee?' 'What?' he says. 'I'll still beatcha.'"[7]

SAYING GOODBYE

Nine days later, on October 24, 1972 Robinson was gone. "I was in the kitchen preparing breakfast," Rachel wrote later. "I looked up, and Jack was rushing down the hallway from the bedroom to the kitchen, obviously headed for me. So I ran to him. He put his arms around me, said 'I love you,' and just dropped to the floor." Robinson was declared dead in the ambulance on the way to the local hospital, but Rachel already knew the truth: "My dearest Jack, my giant, had been struck down, striving to live and loving to the very end."[8]

Robinson's body lay in state for three days before his funeral. A small Harlem funeral home opened its doors to the neighborhood people for eight hours on the first day. "First, they gotta give the poor people a look," one local man told a reporter. "Jackie Robinson gave other black people hope. A beautiful black man."[9] For the next two days, the huge gothic Riverside Church hosted viewings. Hundreds filed past his casket to pay their respects.

On October 27, 2,500 mourners attended Robinson's funeral at Riverside Church. Reporters struggled to list all the luminaries who packed the pews, from Governor Rockefeller to Willie Mays, Joe Louis to Roy Wilkins, and several busloads of schoolchildren besides. Dodgers teammates Jim Gilliam, Don Newcombe, Ralph Branca, Pee Wee Reese, and Joe Black were his pallbearers; Roy Campanella, wheelchair-bound after a paralyzing auto accident, was there as well. Rev. Jesse Jackson gave the eulogy. "When Jackie took the field, something reminded us of our birthright to be free," Jackson said. "In his last dash, Jackie stole home and Jackie is safe."[10]

When the service ended, a mile-long cortege snaked through the city, from Harlem through Bedford-Stuyvesant and out to Cypress Gardens Cemetery in Brooklyn. Tens of thousands stood along the route to say goodbye. Robinson was buried in the borough that had welcomed him so warmly, beside the son he had lost too soon.

In the months and years following his death, public schools jostled for the right to name themselves after Robinson. Rachel set up a foundation in his name to support promising young minority men and women through college and beyond; since 1973, the Jackie Robinson Foundation has given more than 1,100 students scholarships, mentoring relationships, and networking opportunities. A statue of Robinson and Reese, standing proudly together as teammates, was erected in 2005 at Brooklyn's minor-league ballpark, a symbol of unity and understanding that resonates decades after the gesture that inspired it. The U.S. Congress bestowed its highest honor, the Congressional Gold Medal, upon Robinson that same year. A Brooklyn-to-Queens highway was given Robinson's name, as was the rotunda in the New York Mets' new ballpark, set to open in 2009.

The tributes have been many, but the essence of Robinson—his strength, his fierceness, his passion, and his sacrifice—remains so powerful that statues and scholarships pale beside the memory of the man himself. "Jackie was a man who would do anything to help one of his own," said Gene Benson, who knew Robinson only briefly as his roommate on the Negro Leaguers' Venezuelan barnstorming tour of 1945, but who fully grasped the enormity of his life's work. "That was his secret, you understand? He went out and gave his life for black athletes."[11]

NOTES

1. Leonard Koppett, "Ex-Stars Back Reserve Clause Change," *New York Times*, May 22, 1970, p. 22.

2. Jackie Robinson, *I Never Had It Made* (New York: Ecco, 1995), p. 226.

3. Sharon Robinson, *Stealing Home* (New York: HarperPerennial, 1997), p. 176.

4. *California Daily Bruin*, February 2, 1979. Cited in Arnold Rampersad, *Jackie Robinson: A Biography* (New York: Ballantine Books, 1998), p. 457.

5. Rampersad, *Jackie Robinson*, p. 459.

6. Carl E. Prince, *Brooklyn's Dodgers: The Bums, the Borough, and the Best of Baseball* (New York: Oxford University Press, 1996), p. 140. However, another observer said that A's slugger Reggie Jackson visited Robinson's box to tell him, "You've always been my hero," and that Reds players including Johnny Bench and Pete Rose asked Robinson to sign balls for them in the home clubhouse after the game.

7. David Falkner, *Great Time Coming: The Life of Jackie Robinson from Baseball to Birmingham* (New York: Simon and Schuster, 1995), p. 342.

8. Rachel Robinson, with Lee Daniels, *Jackie Robinson: An Intimate Portrait* (New York: Harry N. Abrams, 1996), p. 216.

9. Steve Cady, "A Day for Harlem to Pay Its Respect," *New York Times*, October 26, 1972, p. 51.

10. Steve Cady, "Jackie Goes Home to Brooklyn," *New York Times*, October 28, 1972, p. 25.

11. Falkner, *Great Time Coming*, p. 124.

APPENDIX

Jackie Robinson's Batting Statistics

Year	Team	Games	At Bats	Runs	Hits	Doubles	Triples	Home Runs	Runs Batted In	Walks	Stolen Bases	Strike-outs	Hit By Pitch	Batting Average	On Base Percentage	Slugging Average
1947	Dodgers	151	590	125	175	31	5	12	48	74	29	36	9	.297	.383	.427
1948	Dodgers	147	574	108	170	38	8	12	85	57	22	37	7	.296	.367	.453
1949	Dodgers	156	593	122	203	38	12	16	124	86	37	27	8	.342	.432	.528
1950	Dodgers	144	518	99	170	39	4	14	81	80	12	24	5	.328	.423	.500
1951	Dodgers	153	548	106	185	33	7	19	88	79	25	27	9	.338	.429	.527
1952	Dodgers	149	510	104	157	17	3	19	75	106	24	40	14	.308	.440	.465
1953	Dodgers	136	484	109	159	34	7	12	95	74	17	30	7	.329	.425	.502
1954	Dodgers	124	386	62	120	22	4	15	59	63	7	20	7	.311	.413	.505
1955	Dodgers	105	317	51	81	6	2	8	36	61	12	18	3	.256	.378	.363
1956	Dodgers	117	357	61	98	15	2	10	43	60	12	32	3	.275	.382	.412
Career 10 Years		1,382	4,877	947	1,513	273	54	137	734	740	197	291	72	.311	.409	.474

FURTHER READING

BOOKS

Barra, Allen. *Clearing the Bases: The Greatest Baseball Debates of the Last Century*. New York: St. Martin's Press, 2002.

The Baseball Encyclopedia, Ninth Edition. New York: Macmillan, 1984.

Dorinson, Joseph and Joram Warmund, eds. *Jackie Robinson: Race, Sports, and the American Dream*. Armonk, NY: M.E. Sharpe, 1998.

Durocher, Leo with Ed Linn. *Nice Guys Finish Last*. New York: Simon and Schuster, 1975.

Erskine, Carl. *What I Learned From Jackie Robinson*. New York: McGraw-Hill, 2005.

Eskenazi, Gerald. *The Lip: A Biography of Leo Durocher*. New York: Morrow, 1993.

Falkner, David. *Great Time Coming: The Life of Jackie Robinson from Baseball to Birmingham*. New York: Simon and Schuster, 1995.

Getz, Mike. *Brooklyn Dodgers and Their Rivals, 1950–1952*. Brooklyn, NY: Montauk Press, 1999.

James, Bill and Rob Neyer. *The Neyer/James Guide to Pitchers*. New York: Simon and Schuster, 2004.

Kahn, Roger. *The Boys of Summer*. New York: Perennial Library, 1987.

Lamb, Chris. *Blackout: The Untold Story of Jackie Robinson's First Spring Training*. Lincoln, NE: University of Nebraska Press, 2004.

Mann, Arthur. *The Jackie Robinson Story*. New York: Grosset and Dunlap, 1951.

Mays, Willie and Lou Sahadi. *Say Hey: The Autobiography of Willie Mays*. New York: Simon and Schuster, 1988.

Paige, LeRoy (Satchel). *Maybe I'll Pitch Forever*. Garden City, NY: Doubleday, 1962.

Palmer, Pete and Gary Gillette, eds. *The Baseball Encyclopedia*. New York: Barnes and Noble, 2004.

Prince, Carl E. *Brooklyn's Dodgers: The Bums, the Borough, and the Best of Baseball*. New York: Oxford University Press, 1996.

Rampersad, Arnold. *Jackie Robinson: A Biography*. New York: Ballantine Books, 1998.

Robinson, Jackie. *Baseball Has Done It*. Brooklyn, NY: Ig Publishing, 2005.

Robinson, Jackie. *I Never Had It Made*. New York: Ecco, 1995.

Robinson, Rachel with Lee Daniels. *Jackie Robinson: An Intimate Portrait*. New York: Harry N. Abrams, 1996.

Robinson, Sharon. *Promises to Keep: How Jackie Robinson Changed America*. New York: Scholastic Press, 2004.

Robinson, Sharon. *Stealing Home*. New York: HarperPerennial, 1997.

Rogosin, Donn. *Invisible Men: Life in Baseball's Negro Leagues*. New York: Atheneum, 1983.

Rowan, Carl T., with Jackie Robinson. *Wait Till Next Year*. New York: Random House, 1960.

Simon, Scott. *Jackie Robinson and the Integration of Baseball*. Hoboken, NJ: John Wiley, 2002.

Stout, Glen and Dick Johnson. *Jackie Robinson: Between the Baselines*. San Francisco: Woodford Press, 1997.

Tygiel, Jules. *Baseball's Great Experiment: Jackie Robinson and His Legacy*, expanded edition. New York: Oxford University Press, 1997.

Ward, Geoffrey C. and Ken Burns. *Baseball: An Illustrated History*. New York: Alfred A. Knopf, 1994.

Williams, Pat with Mike Sielski. *How to Be Like Jackie Robinson: Life Lessons from Baseball's Greatest Hero*. Deerfield Beach, FL: Health Communications Inc., 2004.

ARTICLES

Conklin, William R. "Jackie Robinson Chock Full o'Poise as Executive," *New York Times*, March 9, 1958, p. S4.

Hamill, Pete. "The Year of Years," *New York Daily News*, October 9, 2005, pp. 100–103.

Lardner, John. "Reese and Robinson: Team Within a Team," *New York Times Magazine*, September 9 1949, pp. 17–19.

Malcolm X. "Malcolm X's Letter," *New York Amsterdam News*, November 30, 1963, p. 1.

Oursler, Fulton. "Rookie of the Year," *Reader's Digest*, February 1948, pp. 34–38.

Reese, Pee Wee. "What Jackie Robinson Meant to an Old Friend," *New York Times*, July 17 1977, p. 52.

Robinson, Jackie. "What's Wrong with Negro Baseball," *Ebony*, June 1948, pp. 16–18.

Robinson, Jackie. "Now I Know Why They Boo Me!" *Look*, January 15, 1955, pp. 22–28.

Robinson, Jackie. "A Kentucky Colonel Kept Me in Baseball," *Look*, February 8, 1955, pp. 82–90.

Robinson, Jackie. "Your Temper Can Ruin Us!" *Look*, February 22, 1955, pp. 78–87.

Robinson, Jackie. "Malcolm X and Adam Powell," *New York Amsterdam News*, November 16, 1963, p. 1.

Robinson, Jackie. "Jackie Robinson Again Writes to Malcolm X," *New York Amsterdam News*, December 14, 1963, p. 1.

Robinson, Mack. "My Brother Jackie," *Ebony*, July 1957, pp. 75–82.

Sailer, Steve. "How Jackie Robinson Desegregated America," *National Review*, April 8 1996, pp. 38–41.

Tuttle, Dennis. "The Day Racism Hit Home," *USA Today Baseball Weekly*, October 26–31 1995, pp. 26–27.

Tygiel, Jules. "The Court-Martial of Jackie Robinson," *American Heritage*, September 1984, pp. 34–39.

Weaver, Bill L. "The Black Press and the Assault on Professional Baseball's 'Color Line,' October, 1945-April, 1947," *Phylon*, Winter 1979, pp. 303–317.

Young, A. S. "Doc." "The Jackie Robinson Era," *Ebony*, November 1955, pp. 152–156.

Young, A. S. "Doc." "How Sports Helped Break the Color Line," *Ebony*, September 1963, pp. 114–118.

NEWSPAPERS

New York Amsterdam News
New York Daily News
New York Herald Tribune
New York Post
The New York Times
The Sporting News
USA Today Baseball Weekly
Washington Post

WEB SITES

Baseball Almanac. http://www.baseball-almanac.com

BaseballLibrary.com. http://baseballlibrary.com

Baseball Reference. http://www.baseball-reference.com

Library of Congress: Baseball and Jackie Robinson. http://memory.loc.gov/ammem/collections/robinson

INDEX

About the Author

MARY KAY LINGE is a freelance writer and editor who specializes in popular reference and nonfiction. She is the author of *Willie Mays: A Biography* (2005).

5/12
8

12/15   6/17   5/19
20   20   27